Olive S England

Ceres

A Harvest Home Festival and Other Poems

Olive S England

Ceres
A Harvest Home Festival and Other Poems

ISBN/EAN: 9783744711500

Printed in Europe, USA, Canada, Australia, Japan

Cover: Foto ©Thomas Meinert / pixelio.de

More available books at **www.hansebooks.com**

CERES

A HARVEST HOME FESTIVAL,

AND

OTHER POEMS, ESSAYS, ETC.

BY

MRS. OLIVE S. ENGLAND,

———

SALEM, OREGON:
THE E. M. WAITE PRINTING COMPANY.
1893.

CONTENTS.

THE FESTIVAL OF CERES 11
The Indian Woman..33
June and Music..37
Friendship True..44
Divided 46
United 48
The Heart of My Love....................................49
Parting..50
Expectation...51
Opportunity..53
The Violet's Love.......................................54
The End Crowns the Work.................................55
Baby Hands 56
Hartsease...58
A Song of the Soul......................................59
The Out-Going Ships....................................60
A Common Theme—Home...................................62
Imagination...63
Christmas Echoes..63
The Moon and Star.......................................66
Dedication—Unity Church...............................67
True Baptism..68
Aspiration 69
A Sonnet 70
Adelia..70
KNOWLEDGE 77
ONLY A BABY...97
THE AESTHETIC 101

PREFACE.

This little volume is strictly an Oregon production. It has been written, printed and bound in Salem, Oregon. If it should attract the attention of a few readers, they might ask: "Well what of it?" But so they might of thousands of other things at this great exhibition, and if through dread of criticism, exhibitors had failed to send things here, the greatest fair the world has ever seen would have been a complete failure. This volume has been compiled and prepared on two weeks' notice, only, at the solicitation of anauthor friend, Mrs. F. F. Victor, who desired to see Oregon's literary productions at the Columbian Exposition.

The poems and addresses, which are here collected together, were in a very chaotic state, from which I have hardly had time to rescue them. Whether I could have done better, if I had taken more time for preparation, I do not know. I cherish self-esteem enough to think I could; but I am well aware that we often overrate our own ability.

The Festival of Ceres, is published at the suggestion of Miss Susan B. Hale, the sister of Edward Everett Hale. Edward Everett Hale, in an address in the Auditorium, in Chicago, said: that he believed every person in that vast audience had written verses. While versifying is probably not so universal as the illustrious preacher asserted, yet is more common than the general public believe. It is like the ailments of our childhood, a disease common to all. Some have it mildly, while with some it goes severely. I am one of the latter.

For this my first attempt at a book, I hope my frinds will have charity. If one does not depend upon literary efforts for a livelihood, there can be but two other things to fear— lack of experience, and lack of ability to write something that others will care to read. It is more than probable that this little book will be gored by *both* horns.

But I am resolved, no matter what fate may have in store for it, to send it forth, strong in the conviction that it is a "plucky" little thing, though quiet and retiring in its pretentions, and if it merits oblivion, all right. We're used to it, my book and I.

THE AUTHOR.

THE FESTIVAL OF CERES.

CHARACTERS.

CERES, Goddess of Heaven and Earth, also of the Harvest.

SPRING, - - - - - - - { March April May

SUMMER, - - - - - - { June July August

AUTUMN, - - - - - - - { September October November

WINTER, - - - - - - { December January February

CERES.

ACT I.

SLOW MARCH MUSIC.

*Curtain rises, revealing at one side of stage the altar of Ceres,
a little distance in front a seat or throne. Enter priestess
swinging censer from which rises clouds of incense. The
priestess is followed by six vestal virgins, who are slowly
and softly chanting hymn to Ceres (tune Lord's Prayer).*

Chant :

We call upon the great Ceres, in song we call. We ask
thy blessing on the harvest. We praise thee, thou giver of
the oats, of wheat, of all the golden grain ; of corn, of wine,
and for all the blessings thou dost bestow. We burn incense on thy altar that thou mayest ever bless the earth.
Let the light of thy countenance shine upon us. In the
splendor of thy graciousness, come. Bless the earth and
the fullness thereof, Giver of the Harvest Home.

*As they chant they range themselves, three on each side of
altar while priestess pours incense on altar. Enter Ceres,
standing on car to which winged dragons are attached seeming to draw it. As scene parts and Ceres enters, vestals
fall upon their faces. Ceres steps from car, waves burning
torch which she holds in right hand, over vestals, saying,
"Arise." She then pauses before altar, on step of throne.*

Ceres :

From the bright home of the immortal gods I come to celebrate my festival of harvest home. Come forth! Come forth! O powerful servants of my work ; I would know what offerings ye bring to the fullness of the year. Come, thou first and fairest, gentle Ostera, angel of Spring. Come, with thy attendant months, thy offerings bring.

Enter Ostera.

Ostera :

I am Ostera, the angel of spring;
I call ! resurrection to all things I bring :
The Easter awakening from Winter's cold breath ;
The sweet, tender buds I rescue from death.
Midway 'twixt the Winter and Summer I stand
And bring you an off'ring of each in my hand.
Come, March, son of Mars, with the winds in thy train,
Thy off'ring seems cruel, but is not in vain.

March (Mars should be dressed in long black robes, and as he sings should wave robes):

Blow, ye wild winds, blow, blow, blow.
Yet Winter retreats wherever I go.
But after me cometh with sunshine and tears,
Aphrodite, coquetting with hopes and with fears.

Enter April as Venus (March addresses her).

Fair April, how fickle, inconstant thou art.
Of coquetry full.   Ah, hast thou no heart?
Yet something so winsome, so bright in thy smile,
Like laughter and tears on the face of a child.
Like sunbeams, like raindrops, thy clouds come and go.
Shall I trust thee, fair April?   Depend on thee?   No.

April :

But know that I open the buds and the flowers;
Delight with my sunshine, impearl with my showers;
I bring you the birds whose soft downy wings
Gleam bright through the forests as sweetly they sing.
I am Aphrodite, as Venus best known ;
Born of the ocean's salt spray and white foam.
To island of Cyprus in seashell of green,
Was wafted at birth bright April's fair queen ;
I landed, and lo! on that lovely green isle
The flowers burst forth, the Spring's fairest smile.

Spring :

Well, April, thou'rt welcome, if sad or if gay,
E'en tho' mingling March clouds with the sunshine of
    May.

Enter May (Spring addressing her).

My beautiful May, what bringest thou to the great
Ceres, goddess of the earth?

May :

I, the Goddess Maia, bring you pleasure and mirth, and
the butterflies and bees, and also many flowers. The butterflies have ever been the emblems of freed souls, by
Psyche sent to adorn thy festival. The bees are emblematical of industry, that by labor gathereth the sweets from
the flowers that bloom along the paths of life. Accept, O
Ceres, these, my offerings, and I would that most graciously
you look upon my festival, for there pleasure reigns
supreme. That scene of mirth and beauty now behold!
Scene parts revealing May-pole dance. **Curtain.**

ACT II.

Curtain rises to martial music.   Enter Ceres, waves wand of poppies.

Ceres:

Come! queenly Summer, delay not; I long to behold thy resplendent face.

Enter six little girls singing an ode to summer, also bearing garlands of flowers. As they cease singing, Herald of Summer, little girl with beautiful garlands steps forward, saying :.

She comes with music and garlands. Already her spice-laden breath fills the air. Already her zephyrs blow soft o'er the hills. Summer, in all her glorious beauty is on the threshold.

Enter to music, Summer passing between rows of girls wtih garlands.

Summer :

I come from the land where the sunshine is king ;
There is music of fountains, bees hum, birds sing;
There are lilies and roses, and golden-hued flowers;
There beauty reposes 'neath spice-laden bowers.
In the kingdom of Summer we are happy and gay ;
'Tis a fair land of beauty where Love holdeth sway.
You shall hear the sweet music that Summer can bring.

Come, Orpheus; Apollo, thy sweetest strains sing.

Enter Orpheus and Apollo with guitar and mandolin; enter June as Juno.

And here is sweet Juno, so stately and fair,
Go, offer to Ceres thy tribute most rare.

June:

Great Ceres, sister goddess, I come at command,
All crowned with the lillies of sweet Summer-land.
My fairies are dancing e'en now in the light
Of the great silver moon that is shining so bright.

Scene opens, fairies dancing around fairy queen, seated on throne.

June:

Look thou, on that scene, my fairies at play ;
Lovely the offerings I bring you to-day. .

Ceres :

The grace, innocence and beauty of thy offering is indeed beyond compare, and such scenes are well pleasing to the Gods. But where is thy sister July ?

June:

Behold she comes! The great Goddess of Liberty; the best beloved of all upon earth.

July (as Goddess of Liberty):

Most gracious deity, I shall give you the noblest and best. Judge not harshly on first appearance, I know that thou art wise and just, and so fear not to bring to thee my offering. Earth has changed much in all the intervening years since that golden age when the great gods came, and walked, talked, and dwelt among men. Thou knowest *I* have always dwelt upon this earth, because my power as liberator has ever been most needed, and still is needed. He who shall come at my bidding is not of thy race, O, goddess, but O, listen to his plea, for to him and his countryman, my mouth is most sacred. (*She calls.*) "Brother Jonathan, come!"

(Orchestra strikes up Yankee Doodle, enter Brother Jonathan whistling Yankee Doodle.)

Ceres, *(startled):*

Brother Jonathan! No such name was ever known to the immortal gods; whence comest though, who art thou!

Brother J. (Looks around, then places foot on altar; elbow on knee; addresses Ceres, who is much agitated at desecration of her altar.):

Ceres, jest you rest easy; I know what I'm abeout; mebby I haint deoun with them ar immortal gods, and mebby I am. *(Straightens up for speech.)* Dew yeou know anything abeout the Fourth of July? George Washington? *E pluribus unium?* Uncle Sam, the American eagle? Of course you might have associated with the Goddess of Liberty some, as she is your kind ; but there's a few others of our old fore-mothers and fore-fathers shan't be slighted ef I kin tell their story, and I reckon I kin. Pshaw, Ceres! Your edication is all run deoun and haint worth nothin' ef you don't know abeout them. I might hev showed you the picter of George Washington as he was took as a mason. In that he appears at his best. His face is cam and serene. One hand, which guided the Ship of State safely into the port of National Independence, is stretched forth in benediction, and the other holds a gavel, which is as near like a hatchet as it can be made. He was "took" with a dish-apron on jist to please Marthy, (some folks think his apron means something about masonry, but it don't.) It is to show that he was not too "stuck up" to help Marthy wash the dishes, His apron does seem to have a considerable uv fringe, and tuckers and firills on it but they all mean something good, or you wouldn't ketch 'em on him. His principles struck deep ; laid holt of the bed-rock, went clean down to the underpinnin' of things. When he was a little kid his pappy bought him a hatchet to split kindlin' wood with, but the fust thing he used it fur was to chop out the underpinnin' from the ash-hopper, so it couldn't leach off no lie. Oh, I tell you he loved the truth. The same day he busted a hole in his mother's soap kittle, 'cause lie *biled down, concentrated lie*, he couldn't stand. His father had an English cherry tree, growin' out by the piazzay, and though George had at diffeeent times dressed up in British regimentals and faught the Injuns when they tried to steal cherries, yet he hated that tree. So, one day he took his hatchet and began choppin' it down. Every blow meant something: First, he chopped through the bark—which was emblematical of the bark of oppression which sort of hidebound the American colonies and which was cut assunder by the hatchet of George Washington. Every blow was a blow at lies, and that is the reason there is so much *blow* about American citizens now. Little did George think that every blow of his hatchet would ring all around the world, and echo down through all the advancing centuries, proclaiming freedom. But it has. If George had not cut down that tree American politicians might never have become pure and truthful as they are now.

O, what a pity George could not have been in the garden of Eden, and chopped down the tree of knowledge, of good and of *evil*, before the apples were ripe. For I know those apples were *green*, and sort of soured on our fore-parents, Adam and Eve. Anyhow, if George had been there with his hatchet, it would have saved the rest of us from a heap of nonesense and a lot of religious colic. Well, however, the eagle sat on the gable-end of the smoke-house, singin' Hail Columbia to cheer George while he made the chips fly. When the tree fell the eagle screamed out at him, that as he must be about tuckered out, if he would attend to other pressin' matters, she would attend to the *hatch-it* hereafter, as it was more in her line of business; and she did. Nobody could *shew* her away until she got ready to go, either. Finally, she took that tree in her tallons, just as you see it in the coat of arms, and flew to her eyrie on the lonely, beetling crag of the Rock of Independence, and clawed it all to pieces and used some of the pieces to build into her nest. O, Ceres, you had orto seen that old bird's nest! It was the most outlandishest nest ever built under the sun. There was something in it from every clime, and she made some of *them climb* too ; hence the solubrity of the *climate* (climb it.)

In that nest are germs from Germany, franchise from France, bells from Belgium, hop-poles and polecats from Poland, chills and agur from Chili, beaux from Bohemia, rushes from Russia, switches from Switzerland, sandwiches from the Sandwich Islands, china asters from China, pans from Japan, guinea hens from Guinea, hollers from Holland, Canada thistles from Canada, gum arabic from Arabia, hungry folks from Hungary, taller candles from Greece, Indians from India, ideas from Idaho, biscuits from the Bay of Biscay and turkey-feathers from Turkey. When she got her nest all done she named it *E Pluribus Unum, Sic Semperatus* Alpaca Holly Hock, cause she knew it was one formed of many, and also that we would need a national flower, and besides, she was a clever old bird and

understood Latin jist as well as any language under the
sun. Of course the Eagle made a little mistake to disturb
George before he had chopped the tree down root and
branch, but the best of us make mistakes. History tells us
that that cherry-tree stump "is still there" and sends up a
few shoots occasionally. On this account Americans might
possibly lie once in a while, but I don't think so.

Philosophers tell us no stream can rise above its source.
If there ever was a pure stream started in a straight and
narrer source, it was the steam of national honor and truth
started by the blows of the hatchet of George Washington,
but it got to meanderin' off down the mountain side, and
the further off it got, the worse it meandered. Upon this
subject you should muse, Ceres, and muse deeply.

Ceres, I'm agoin' to tell you about our flag. We allers
thought some of you old goddesses got it up, in heaven.
Somebody must have had a streaky time a gittin' it up.
There's a streak of red, and a streak of white, and a whole
patch of blue. The white and blue represent the truth and
purity of America's politics and politicians. The red is the
emblem of the blood shed by America's heroes, a keepin'
of 'em pure. But I don't see how that flag pole can point
without a blush straight up to that heaven from whence
came the true, blue ground-work of those pure, white, free
stars until American women are allowed to help the Eagle
and the Goddess of Liberty hold up that pole. For we all
know that the afore-mentioned, the Goddess and the Eagle,
were two very sensible females, who were right on hand in
the start to help George with this Republic.

After the Republic wuz got up, the Eagle heard the

British Lion a roarin', and she flew at him and clawed his
eyes out, and Yankee Doodle Dandy got drunk on tea and
they flung him overboard in Boston harbor, but he jist
swam out a whistlin' his own immortal tune ; George Washington waded the Delaware, with the snow clean up to his
armpits, and the ice and slush a runnin' like all tarnation,
and the same night the old Britishers took a cold which
settled into a steddy rheumatiz, which is still a grindin'
'em. But I'm ahead uv my story and sort of mixed up a
little, but Ceres, them's facts all the same.

And when George's father found the tree cut down he
asked George if he done it with his little sharp-aiged
hatchet. "You won't lick me if I tell the truth, will you,"
asked George. "I don't lick for nothin' but lies," yelled
the old man. Then to save hisself from gettin' licked for
cuttin' the tree, Georgie said : "Father, I did. I cannot
tell a lie." Of course George wuzzent to blame fur tellin'
the truth, coz history says he couldn't lie. Then his pappy
embraced him, and they mingled their tears on the same
bandannar handkercher (that is to say the old man cried
and wiped Georgie's nose).

The war of the Revolution broke loose—the war of 1812
wuz a brewin'—the war of the Rebellion got ripe—the
Goddess of Liberty ragged out in red, white and blue and
flirted a little with Uncle Sam. Yankee Doodle gave three
whoopin' cheers fur *E Pluribus Unum, Sic Semperatus*
Alpaca Holly Hock, and we became a free and glorious
Republic with fire-crackers ripe at all seasons of the year,
and the Eagle done the yellin'.

Now, Ceres, I'll be plain with you, if we're not daown

on ycour list of them old gods, I shall allers think we'd ort to be.

Ceres, much agitated, arises :

Brother Jonathan, thy noble countryman, that bright hero, George Washington's name shall forevermore be placed upon the scroll of fame, and high upon Olympus' shining crest shall thy country's deeds be sung by heavenly choirs. The flag of thy native land shall evermore unfurl its shining folds and be caressed by every breeze that blows, and kissed by the sunshine's golden flame. Thy glorious Eagle shall now, and always conquering bear aloft thy glorious coat of arms in triumph. And listen! Brother Jonathan, thine own illustrious name shall stand first upon the list of the immortal gods !!

Brother Jonathan rushes up to Ceres, grasps her hand, saying :

Put it there, pard.

Goddess of Liberty pats Brother Jonathan on the back. Brother Jonathan then links Goddess of Liberty's arm in his own, both exit, he whistling Yankee Doodle.

Ceres to Summer :

Summer, call forth thy other month, thy glorious king.

Summer :

Great August, come !

Enter August, as Helios, God of the Sun.

August :

Summer, my queen, I am here at thy bidding, I, the firemonth, Great Helios, God of the Sun. From this cup of gold I pour the sunshine over all the earth. *He carries*

gold cup in which gold thread of curled wire are concealed,
which, when he turns cup upside down, fall to the stage. My
fierce beams ripen fruit and grain. 'Tis my offering—may
it prove well pleasing in thy sight. I also bring you the
music of harvesters singing as they reap the yellow grain.

Scene opens revealing harvest scene.

ACT III.

Ceres :

Summer has gone ; but where is bounteous Autumn, my
beautiful, my favorite season. I would behold thy face,
best beloved, come! Great Ceres commands!

Enter Autumn, dressed in scarlet :

I have come! I am Autumn! Cast off the dead roses!
I am decked in the robes that are fairer than all,
For nature is brightest before she reposes,
E'er the wintry winds come, or the early snows fall.

I have come in the granduer of flame and of glory,
To fulfill all the promise of Summer and Spring,
E'er my red banners fade; e'er my crown shall turn hoary;
Accept ye the fruitage and blessings I bring.

Come ! Come in thy glory, immortal September,
Bring gold of the harvest in thy gen'rous hand,
The gifts that ye bring, shall all men remember,
As far the most precious brought forth in the land.

Enter September, bearing sheaves of grain which she lays at Ceres' feet.

September :

 Our country is blest, 'tis the greatest and grandest—
  What more would we ask, if we could, of the gods?
 Kind nature is lavish of her choicest blessings,
  Which springeth like magic from Oregon's sod.
 The most brilliant gems on her bosom reposes,
  For her mines with their riches begin to unfold;
 Her plains, and her mountains, her rivers and forests;
  Her cereals abounding all freighted with gold.

Autumn :

 October, come forth! thy sister is waiting,
  O, bring us rich draughts of life's purple wine,
 Bring banners of Autumn, I long to behold them;
  Bring fruits that are luscious—bring *all* that is mine.

October, bearing fruits :

 Great Autumn, I come! all clothed in the splendor
  That Nature in beauty now weaves 'round the year:
 Here are fruits of the vine, I bring you so luscious,
  'Tis Nature's last tribute e'er Winter appear.
 From my brows, when my garland of spendor shall wither,
  It shall melt into beauty that Winter shall give,
 My leaves that are scarlet, in cold winds now quiver,
  Yet in new forms of being and wonder shall live;
 In the buds of the spring-time, in garlands of summer,
  Eternal progression! but never decay.
 In grain that shall ripen, in fruits growing mellow,
  My bright forms are changing forever and aye.

I bring golden dreams of soft Indian summer,
That come to this earth at the change of the year—
And e'en gods may dream! Behold! O great Ceres!
Bright vision, of beauty all-glorious, appear!

*She claps her hands, scene opens, reveals statuary and posing
lasting several moments. This can be made exceedingly
beautiful by well-drilled performers and soft, low, sweet
music. Scenes close one moment here, rises immediately.*

Autumn:
Come forth! November, November.

Enter November.

I come from the shade, November, November,
I come, and red Autumn's best tribute I bring.
'Tis hearts that are full of blessed thanksgiving
For all that the year in its fullness doth bring.

Scene parts revealnig Thanksgiving dinner scene.

November:
See! Beloved Goddess, Earth's children are happy,
behold feasting and mirth. The true thanksgiving comes
from happy hearts; happy in the knowledge that this is
the golden year of Oregon's prosperity.

ACT IV.

Ceres:
I now call fair, cold Winter. Come Winter, that the
circle of the year may be complete. Come, from the dis-

tant land of the midnight sun! Come, on the rosy chariot
of the flaming Aurora Borealis! May the freezing north-
wind speed thee o'er thy icy road !

*Enter Queen of Winter, accompanied by Jack Frost, music of
sleigh-bells.*

Winter :
  Great goddess, this servant that cometh with me,
    Cold, cold December, not welcome is he,
  For the life-force of Nature is locked by his key.
    He locks in a prison each bud, leaf and flower,
  Sends blight, desolation from his icy tower.
    In my home, in the far-frozen caves of the north,
  Weave I garments of snow, make jewels of frost.
    Jack Frost is my servant o'er mountains and lea,
  He spreads my fair garments, so lovely to see.

Jack·Frost, as December :
  When brightly is burning the fire on the hearth,
  A delicate lace-work I weave o'er the earth;
  Though locking in prisons the flowers of Spring,
  More beautiful far are the blossoms I bring,
  They are born of the breath of the Angel of Snow,
  I scatter them, scatter them, wherever I go.
  I bind the wild rivers with a glittering chain—
  Until Spring in her tenderness free's them again.

Winter :
  By my crown with its jewels—my magical wand—
  The forces of Nature are safe in his hand,
  For the mystery of life, whatever it be,
  Lives safe in the power invested in me.

December :

Now the festival greatest of all on the earth,
I bring as my offering—judge thou of its worth.

       (*Scene part, reveals Christmas scene.*)

Ceres :

Why, 'tis the old Saturnalia,

December :

             Renewing each year,
Under new name of Chistmas, enjoyments dear.

Winter :

I would call another servant, Janus or January, to whom
is now accorded the honor of being the first month in the
year.

Ceres :

Janus Bifrons? Ah! yes, wave thy jeweled wand.
Summon him with libations of rich wine. Let incense
burn upon my altar. I would that he should'st honor my
festival. Let thy high-priest summon him.

*Winter signs to December to burn incense, and pours wine over
altar, saying :*

Come, Janus, thou keeper of the eternal doors of earth
and heaven.

     Enter Saturn, or Old Father Time, as Old Year.

Old Year :

Stay! E'er he come, I must pass before thy altar. I
must bid farewell and follow the unnumbered years into
that far-off past of which I so soon shall become a part. My

work is ended. I have been a faithful servant. Great Ceres, judge thou my work—all these that have passed before thee are but parts of my work. Come, December, thou goest with me. I go, farewell, farewell.

All on stage solemnly reply, "Farewell, farewell."

Enter January as Janus Bifrons, with two masks or faces on, leading by hand little New Year.

Janus:

I come at thy bidding. I that openeth and shutteth the doors of the year, and also the everlasting doors of high heaven where Great Jupiter sits enthroned in awful majesty. My face looks forth with compassion on the retreating year, who with bowed form and drooping head recedes forever from mortal sight. But I bring to you, O stately Goddess, the infant New Year. I have closed the door upon the Old Year and his finished work. I have opened for the New, whose work begins. O may all the gods propitious be to him, and bounteous giver of earth's most precious things, may thy blessing be upon him that he may faithful prove.

Ceres takes him by the hand and waving wand says, "'Tis done."

Winter:

I have yet another servant who waits without to bring his tribute to thy shrine. February, come!

February as St. Valentine.

February:

What remains for me to offer, where all have brought such bounteous gifts to thee, O, Ceres, Goddess of the Golden

Harvest time; and of all the earth, all, all is thine! We
do but render to thee thine own again. The feast of Purity
which is the event which gave to me my name, is but
founded on a sacred feast which, as thou knowest well, in
the ages gone, was sacred unto thee. But I, Saint Valentine, have dedicated another day, and this to Love. Come,
sweet Love; bring pretty Cupids in, and as thy songs in-
spire men's souls, and captivate all hearts, those pretty
boys of thine may send some arrows home.

*Enter Love with cupids holding up her train; she sings while
cupids pose with drawn bows. As the song is finished enter
Brother Jonathan.*

Brother Jonathan:

Look a here now, February, you and Ceres, and all you
gods and goddesses, you'd better not forget that part of
February belongs to George Washington. I recon he got
in about the 22nd. Git eout, now; yeour kind haint to
be talked abeout the same day as his'n. And he, the
father of this 'ere American Republic—and a full partner
of the bald headed eagle.

*Music starts up Hail Columbia; Ceres takes arm of Brother
J. They lead procession; all performers come out two by
two; grand march.* CURTAIN.

POEMS.

POEMS.

——

THE INDIAN WOMAN.

[The following poem was written at Newport, Yaquina Bay,
Oregon, on the occasion of the death of an Indian Woman named
Annette, who was said to be the most beautiful woman on the
reservation. She was much more refined and better educated
than her companions. Her husband, whom she tenderly loved
had deserted her, and by many was thought to be her murderer.
She had become very melancholly and would wander off alone
by the sea-shore at night, after her work for the day was done.
At the time of her death she was employed at the Ocean House, a
summer resort of Newport. There were many pleasure seekers
at the hotel at the time, and two days after the sad occurrence, at
an amateur entertainment, (the first entertainment ever given at
Newport) given in the parlors of the Ocean House, this poem was
read by its author. Annetta was burried at the Siletz Reservation, eight miles distant from Newport.]

> Found dead ! an Indian woman,
> Found lying on the sand ;
> A dark-haired Indian woman ;
> Yes, murdered on the strand !
>
> A red wound on her dusky throat,
> The seaweed in her hair,
> The moonbeams shining on her face,
> Which once was wondrous fair.
>
> Her soft eyes closed forevermore
> On scenes of life and love,

Shall wake in realms of beauty, in
   That Eden-land above.

Her graceful form but yesterday
   Was bounding o'er the strand—
To-day all cold and silent is,
   A clod upon the sand.

But she an Indian outcast was,
   What careth you and me?
The fate, this dark woman, dead!
   So near the rippling sea.

Not e'en one peal of laughter gay
   Of strollers on the shore,
Shall for one moment be less glad,
   Though she come nevermore.

Her life could not have gladsome been ;
   Her death can't help but be
Much better than her life hath prov'd,
   While dwelling by the sea.

For she was but a lowly one,
   And all she had was life.
But once she had a lover true—
   Though now deserted wife.

The human heart is human still—
   With wild sweet wayward love—
And but an Indian woman, may
   Its deepest passions prove.

For love a thing eternal is—
  And even her dark breast
Had felt its deepest meaning thrill,
  And known its wild unrest.

She said her heart was sorrowful,
  She longed to be at peace,
She strayed down by the waters wild,
  Whose moanings never cease.

The moon rose o'er the mountains high ;
  She saw the golden horn,
Against the purple sky of night,
  Where shining stars are born.

A prayer went forth from dusky lips,
  To him who rules above,
That she might cast the burden off,
  Of unrequited love.

A cloud sailed o'er the moon's fair face,
  The waves rose white and high ;
A shriek rung out upon the night!
  A woman's wild death cry.

      *   *   *   *   *

And so at morn they found her, dead!
  So near the restless sea—
But only an Indian outcast gone ;
  What's that to you and me.

The waves dash wildly on the shore ;
  They wash the blood-stained sands—

Salt waves that leave the sands all clean,
  But not the murd'rer's hands.

Ah! waves, sad waves, that moan and sigh,
  The truth you cannot tell ;
You whispor of that tragedy,
  But keep the secret well.

Ah! does the God of justice sleep ?
  Or shall his power reach—
Requite that humble woman there,
  Found murdered on the beach ?

Will not the law, with mighty arm,
  Her dreadful wrong requite ?
Will justice strive the same for her
  As if her face were white ?

    *   *   *   *   *

Well, let her comrades take her to
  The distant lonely grave;
Beyond the mountains dark and high,
  Beyond the rolling wave.

They started on their journey, as
  The moon rose o'er the sea*—
Whille o'er the hills and valley's deep,
  They bore her tenderly.

The wild waves thundered on the shore,
  While o'er the waters wide,
The winds were sobbing to the stars,
  And far out o'er the tide.

*These Indians would not touch the body of a murdered person until the moon rose.

All nature seemed to grieve for her,
　For she was Nature's child,
A flower that in the forest bloomed—
　Some fairest flowers are wild.

God's flowers of the forest sweet,
　Whose perfumes are so rare
As those that fills the costliest vase,
　Or deck the sunniest hair.

But now with death we leave her clay,
　Within that spirit-land
The soul hath passed of her we mourn,
Found murdered on the strand.

JUNE AND MUSIC.

[A poem delivered before the Musical Alumni of Willamette
University, June 10, 1891.]

The poet license always hath
To sing his songs in any key,
Make use of fact and myth, to make
His poem harmonize with ease;
For fact and myth, together, make
Beliefs of men in every state.
Together, best they please.

And now, kind friends, we ask of you
Attention, while we sing
A song of June and Music's power.
And though new thoughts we may not bring,

'Twill help to while away one hour—
Some good you may receive—
Although this story not believe.

Long, long ago, (we give no dates)
But when this earth was younger far,
E'er Music's instruments were made
As now, or so well played,
E'er *Art* such instruments had strung ;
But Nature's voices—sweeter far—
Forever fill'd the earth with sound
Of melody divine ; whose instruments,
So cunningly devised, have ever been
The highest form of minstrelsy.
Were listened to, with reverence more,
Than since hath Art attained such power.

In that age long since pass'd away.
Bright June in bower of roses rare,
All crowned with lilies sweet and fair,
And beautiful beyond compare,
The Queen of Summer reigned.

Her lovely nymphs at her command,
Brought flowers sweet, from every land,
And shells and pearls from ocean's strand,
Her favor thus to gain.   *o'er*
The West Wind came from the lea,
And told ner tales so sweet ;
He told of islands in the seas,
Of Gardens of Hesperides,
Her golden apples on the trees,

Of spray that dashes wild and free
Where winds and waters meet.

She did not smile — and June can frown,
But said, "One blessing yet I miss,
Not precious things from country, town,
Not gold or germs in earth far down,
Not glist'ning snows from Mount Hood's crown,
Not fragrant breath from islands far,
Nor shining light from distant star,
Can add unto my bliss."

Apollo comes with tuneful lyre,
All strung with strands of golden hair,
While with him all the muses sing,
And at his call, from wooded hills
Come fays and fairies with a will,
And gnomes and sprites from reedy rills,
And bright-hued birds their sweet notes trill
The joy and praise they bring.

Now hearing such sweet harmonies,
The fauns and satyrs dance with ease,
Sweet zephyrs sigh all through the trees,
And gladly lend their softened notes,
As sounds Apollo's witching lyre.
While all the insects softly croon,
And murmuring waters in attune
Go rippling on their way.
The woodland echoes gently blend,
And many charms to music lend.
All Nature's voices wild and gay,

Help swell the merry roundelay,
'Til every tone of music sweet,
Now makes the chorus full, complete,
While all these voices in attune,
Have but one theme, the praise of June.

These sentiments they sing to her :
" We hail you, Summer's sovereign,
The Queen of Beauty evermore.
Around your feet in beauty spring
And bloom the radiant flowers,
And unto you their incense bring.
Whene'er shall reign the month of June,
With perfect days and laughing hours,
When bird and bee, on downy wings,
And all bright dreams that Summer brings,
Proclaim thee Queen of lovely things ;
Who scatterest blessings ev'ry day,
From all thy rosy, leafy bowers,
Does earth her thankful anthems raise."
Apollo's hand across the strings,
With yet more skillful touch he brings;
From heaven leaped down the sacred fire
That warms the heart with wild desire
That music only brings ;
And this the burden of his song.

Where e'er shall reign the month of June,
Shall all the youth throughout the land—
Who shall the intellect expand—
Be crowned with honors and degrees ;
And, all, who in the minds of youth

Instill the principles of truth,
Shall rest from labors; take their ease.
Teachers and pupils, free from care,
Shall seek the balmy mountain air;
The ocean's breath inhale—the balm
Of summer-time—in rest and calm.

But greatest gifts that we can bring
Shall Music be in everything;
The earth be all attuned
With melody, from shore to shore.

Fair June, then took her lilly wreath
And crowned Apollo's brow,
And said: "Not e'en the wealth of June,
With brilliant flowers and sweet perfume;
With halcyon days of light and bloom,
And lang'rous dreams of Summer-time;
Would e'er be sweet without the charm
Of rest, and Music's power."

All through the ages down since then,
Hath these same blessings come to men
In June commencement songs and flowers;
While "sweet young graduates" try their powers;
Reunions come, and then farewell
To Alma Mater, 'round which dwell
The mem'ries sweet that future years
Cannot obliterate.

To us oft comes the smiles and tears
As we recall June-days gone by,
With all they meant to happy youth—

Just starting forth to try life's fate.
And as the years doth intervene,
And life's events come in between,
Will mem'ry, ever glancing back,
Review the scenes—the faces sweet—
That somehow dimmer grow; the feet
That trod these halls, and left no trace,
Whose footsteps echo in the place
Within the chambers of the soul.

And like these youthful ones who stand
Upon the threshold of that land,
The future dimly seen ;
Like fledgeling bird that longs and waits
To spread his untried wings ;
We long for heights we yet shall reach,
And feel the holiness you teach
The soul, O, Music, sweet,
And dream of songs we yet shall sing
When by our better angels taught.

These aspirations of the soul
That hath desire for higher goal.
This life is ever incomplete,
Yet tones of music strangely sweet
Is ever sounding through its pain,
Appeal to us, and not in vain,
From higher source than creeds of men;
For creeds of men would fetter thought,
And cannot satisfy the soul.

For thought an angel is all bright,
That cometh from the world of light
With free unfettered wings,
While to our souls this truth she brings:
It is not how we worship Him,
But so in truth we find our God.
And oft 'tis Music doth reveal
God's truth, man's mysteries would conceal.
God strikes these harps with unseen hand,
Yet we at last shall understand.

The homesick soul this music hears—
It is not heard with mortal ears—
'Tis sound of voices wond'rous dear,
Of those gone forth so fearlessly
To meet the sweet deep mystery
In realms far, silent, yet so near.

And often, when the evening sky
Unfurls his banners golden flame,
Reveals the pathway leading high,
And fills the soul with prophecy
Too vast and deep for human speech;
When breath of June fills all the air
With incense sweet, beyond compare,
Then does the spell that Music brings,
The sacred fire from heaven that came,
Burn in the heart with fervid flame,
Emotions strange like billows roll,
By turns they struggle for the soul
Its mastery to attain.

Our spirits fill'd with sacred thought.
Shall know the lesson it hath taught
Of more than transitory things.
Thus those we love we meet again ;
For all *sweet hopes of better things*
Are but some form of angel wings
That wafts the soul to some fair height,
Whence flow the fountains life and light.
'Tis thus deep wisdom dries all tears ;
Dispels our doubts, and quiets fears ;
And leads us upward to the light
Revealed through Music's subtle power.

FRIENDSHIP TRUE.

I gazed upon her winsome face
    Which glowed with intense feeling ;
How I admired the kindly grace
    Her tender eyes revealing !
I knew that I had met a soul
    Who read aright my mission ;
I knew that to us both had come
    All friendship's full fruition.

Her face is tender, sweet and fair,
    And yet so strong and noble,—
Reveals a friendship that will wear,
    Lend strength in times of trouble.
Few friends will love us with our faults,
    Alas, we all are human,
But this friend loves me as I am,
    Ah, noble love of woman.

How seldom is this life of ours,
　Where jealousy and envy
Oft lurks amidst the fairest flower,
　And poisons feelings friendly.
Do we thus meet with earnest love,
　Which is all free from passion,
The gross and sensual far above,
　O, would it were in fashion.

Friendship, although a golden chain
　That binds fond hearts together,
How easy 'tis to part its links,
　Aye! sunder them forever.
But she is always true to me;
　She makes me nobler, better,
Her friendship is a chain of flowers,
　I love each shining fetter.

She is not rich! nor beautiful!
　And her's a mission lowly,
But yet she is my patron saint,—
　Her influence pure and holy;
And though she claims no special creed,
　She holds a deep communion
With Him who knows the soul's great need,
　Divine, or sadly human.

And, as some sinful penitent
　Before his saint is kneeling,
Pours out his soul in passion's prayer,
　And seeks for God's revealing;

'Tis thus I often go to her,
  Sweet, tangible and human,
And she and I speak heart to heart,
  As woman unto woman.

As Christ had one his "best beloved,"
  Who leaned in trust upon him,
So may we hold some precious friend,
  With special love may crown him.
True friendship is a holy thing,
  Above, beyond all passion ;
It is of that which angels are,
  Alas! 'twere more in fashion.

DIVIDED.

At night, in dreams, I feel thy fond embrace
  I feel thy dewy breath upon my face,
Thy voice so dear, I hear repeat my name,
  With rapture thrills my soul, again, again,
O! darling, surely doubt can never come.
  In faith, true love like rare exotics bloom ;
And yet a flow'r that oft may quickly blow,
  Whose perfume fills the air of dewy eve.

The love that's true, is deathless, like the star
  Whose light illumes the earth from heaven afar,
The flow'r of love a wond'rous fragrance leaves
  Like breath of heav'n some golden censer breathes.
Then shall we cast this lovely thing aside ?
  Destroy this bloom more fair than all beside ?

From out our hearts the tendrils tear away,
  And close our eyes to perfect golden day,
And naught remain but night and withered leaves?

Ah! no! my lover, ev'ry flow'r that blows
  Of love is deathless; like a star it glows.
As life is gliding on, each day, each hour,
  The shining chain of love with firmer pow'r
Will bind true hearts together, welded fast
  With love our God hath linked and such shall last,
Tho' fate 'till death such hearts assunder keep—
  Tho' mountains rise between—the misty deep !
And still shall heart so true, so true remain.

And so my lover, though the mists arise
  And roll all dark between, and blind our eyes,
And dim may seem the promised land so fair—
  Tho' storms arise and chill the balmy air ;
Yet when two hearts shall beat with tend'rest love
  These clouds that rise between their constance prove,
And while this world may sunder'd keep
  These two that need each other, yet to weep
Or sadly moan, will not a vict'ry gain.

But when far out, safe o'er the unknown sea,
  We'll love for aye! Our spirits ever free!
We know, my lover, love gives " bitter sweet "
  When love like ours, so oft must coldly meet,
But patient waiting through the mystic years
  May bring surcease of sorrow, dry the tears
And full fruition bring. Then let us be
  Forever true and noble, and then for you and me
Must come the peace and happiness we seek.

UNITED.

We stood together, Nora,
  The waves were rolling high,
'Twas after years of absence —
  A long and sad good-bye;
The clouds hung o'er the mountain
  The mists rose o'er the sea,
While clouds of doubt about our hearts
  Were dark to you and me.

The waves in low complaining,
  That broke in dashing spray,
Told not of greater anguish
  Than filled our hearts that day;
I think the wild commotion —
  Of troubled, star-lit sea —
Was like the waves of hope and fear,
  And doubt, that swept o'er me.

I clasped your hand, my Nora,
  It trembled at my touch,
A thrill of hope swept o'er me,
  Ah! had I hoped too much?
The waves were surging at our feet,
  Wild tossed the foaming spray,
The tide ebbed out toward other shores,
  We seemed to drift away.

And while the waters surged and moaned,
  We watched the shining waves,

While mem'ry's tide rushed o'er our souls,
　　With hopes of other days;
Forgetting pride and sorrow,
　　And all the years between,
The love of youth came back again,
　　And all we once had been.

We loved! I know, dear Nora,
　　For each a glad surprise
Was felt in that strange meeting.
　　I gazed in your dear eyes
And understood that silence deep;
　　Around us sunshine fell —
The hope of years fulfilled at last,
　　You loved me fond and well.

THE HEART OF MY LOVE.

There are mysteries deep that lie hid in the stars,
　　There are secrets that green billows keep,
But not greater than those in a true woman's heart,
　　Filled with love that is holy and deep.
There are pages whose writing I never may read,
　　In the heart of my love, true and sweet,
For its secrets are deep as those of the stars,
　　Or those hid in the waves at my feet.

But the heart of my darling at last shall unfold,
　　In the light of a passion like mine;
'Tis a beautiful volume I yearn so to read,
　　That the key to the clasp I shall find.

We know the mistake that our hearts once had made
  Are borne out on the stream of the years,
And the dross of a love we once thought to be true
  Is now gone, with its doubts and its fears.

Now, I know, in the dreamy, soft after-glow sweet,
  When the heart's wildest passions all rest,
Is the time when my soul hath the need of you most,
  When our love is the truest and best ;
We have learned the saddest of lessons in life,
  While the years have been drifting away ;
We realize now all that lesson hath cost,
  As we stand here at the close of the day.

The dark night of the past hath been filled with unrest,
  But the sun-light of morning now breaks,
While the glory of hope fills my life with its wine,
  And my spirit a new purpose takes.
See, my love, the dark clouds from the mountains now roll,
  And the mist shall soon rise from the sea,
While the sorrow that clouded my heart is dispelled
  In the sunshine my soul finds in thee.

PARTING.

I'll hear no more the loving words
  That you have spoken oft to me,
The sweetest I have ever heard,
  You've told me by the star-lit sea.

But I must go, my home is there —
  Though gloomy mountains rise between;
Yet shall I hear your tender words,
  Whene're the sun-set's gold shall gleam.

Yes, I must hasten far away,
  For you have woven 'round my life
The woof that by a magic spell,
  Transforms all duty into strife.

And so, farewell! in peace you stay;
  All sorrow I shall take with me;
Yet evr'y western breeze that blows,
  Will waft some tender thought to thee.

EXPECTATION.

Ethel. Ethel, pretty Ethel,
  Gazing o'er the waters blue,
Wond'ring when some ship returning
  Comes to bring her lover true.

Thoughtful Ethel, fair and youthful,
  Wand'ring by the tossing sea,
Gazing out beyond the breakers —
  O'er the deep's immensity.

It all seems a sea of glory,
  Far beyond the foaming spray,
Where, defined the line of breakers,
  Shows where ocean meets the bay.

And I read, my little maiden,
  All your heart most longs to say :
"Will e'er come my ship all laden,
  With a wealth of love some day?"

Yes, far o'er the bounding billow,
  Comes a bark with snowy sail;
Precious treasure that it brings you,
  All your heart shall joyful hail.

For you are a blithesome maiden,
  And the sounding of the sea
Of the life to which you hasten,
  Seems to murmur pleasantly.

And your heart shall go to meet it
  Far out o'er the bounding wave;
All your steps of life shall greet it —
  Walking with it to the grave.

But beware! my darling Ethel,
  All along the shell-strewn shore,
See you not the tangled sea-weed,
  Hear you not the billows roar?

Listen to the deep, wierd music,
  As the waves break at your feet,
Tones of sadness intermingle
  With the tones of hope that greet.

O, my Ethel, happy Ethel,
  Wrecks are cast up by the waves,
Telling true of dire disaster,
  And of lonely ocean graves.

But I think, as o'er the billows,
  Far you gaze with longing eyes,
Soon the "snowy sail" appearing,
  Brings your lover true and wise.

OPPORTUNITY.

O, white-winged ships, that sailed by me
  No cargo brought, none took away,
Say, will you ever come again
  To take my work—forgive my play?
You reached a port whence no return—
  I hear the answer o'er the sea;
Regrets and tears will not avail—
  You sailed to Port Eternity.

But other ships are sailing by,
  They too, may never come again,
And so I'll hail them as they fly,
  Like birds of passage o'er the main.
A warning sound is in the waves,
  And while I listen to its tone,
That echoes through the ocean caves,
  And on the sands so sadly moan.

Resolve to send good cargoes forth
  By ships that anchor soon and sure,
With treasures I have garnered up
  To be kept there safe and secure.
O, white-winged ships, you passed me by,
  And I'll regret it while I live;
Each wave that dashes on the shore,
  Will bring regrets, and make me grieve.

THE VIOLET'S LOVE.

Close to earth a violet blossomed,
　Yet it raised its modest eyes,
Upward gazed through cloudless ether,
　Drawing color from the skies ;
While its golden heart so tiny,
　Like a star that shone above,
Where the violet gazed with longing,
　'Till 'twas like its shining love.
But it sighed : " My humble mission
　Is to bloom one little hour,
While fair star, thou art immortal,
　Grand thy work is, great thy power,
Brief my day of scent and blossom,
　Filled with dewy tears my eyes ;
Yet I long to be immortal,
　Like the stars in purple skies.

Mine is such a lowely mission,
　Just to breathe an incense sweet,
Here, amid the humble grasses,
　Trampled down by careless feet."
Soon there came a gentle zephyr,
　Sent from lands so fair and far,
Wafting fragrance from the violet
　Off'ring incense to the star.

From the star the faintest shimmer —
　Just one little golden ray.
Touched the heart that dearly lov'd it,
　Then went wand'ring on its way.

Soon there came a careless footstep,
  Treading on the violet blue,
Crushing all its fragile petals,
  Trampling on its heart so true.

Then the summer air of evening,
  Bore the violets dying sigh
Upward floating, through blue ether
  Where its star begemmed the sky.

So 'tis well we learn a lesson
  From the violet, true and wise,
Though to earth our life-work keeps us,
  Our ideals mount the skies ;
Hearts reflect the lights they worship,
  Whether sun, or moon, or star,
What we long for, we attain to,
  Though above us bright and far.

THE END CROWNS THE WORK.

[Class Motto : Written for Senior Class, Willamette University.]

To-day we leave thee, Alma Mater —
  Mingling tears of joy and grief,
We now take up a broader life-work,
  It may be long, it may be brief ;
Tho' our work may be unfinished,
  As we feel it is to-day,
Yet our Father knows our efforts,
  And our labor day by day.

Life is work as well as sunshine,
　Patient work thro' days and years
That wins the crown for which we're striving,
　Rewards the toil, the strife and tears.
So, all thro' this life's swift journey,
　Where'er works and faith be found,
Will reward tho' slow in coming,
　Sometime evr'y effort crown.

When the sheaves of life are garner'd,
　When the harvest work is done,
The tired reapers, sad and weary,
　Seek the crown their brows have won ;
Shall the prize for which we labor'd,
　Diploma from the Father's hand
Be given us, a shining guerdon,
　Passport to the better land.

BABY HANDS.

These baby hands, soft baby hand,
　What power for weal or woe,
May not one day these hands command ?
　No power of mine may know.
You're chubby, fair and dimpled now,
　And frail as any flower —
You yet may lead an army on
　To victory, death or power.

These little hands so pure and sweet,
　May guide the Ship of State
Through troubled waters wide and deep,

Oppression's chains may break ;
May point the way to heaven's throne,
Within the gates of pearl,
May stretch in benediction forth,
Above a kneeling world.

These little hands! a shudder thrills
Within this heart of mine,
What if—but I brook no *if's*
A future grand is thine.
What have I said ? O, Father, dear,
Forgive my wayward heart,
If but in worldly victories,
I'd give my child a part.

These hands may work a fearful curse,—
The future's veiled from me ;
Temptation's dark may overcome
Without true grace from thee.
Then may thy grace to him be given,
May every cause of right
Have aid of these two little hands,—
Then work them with thy might.

Well, baby dear, these thoughts of mine,—
Mere castles in the air,—
Have filled my soul with longings deep,
With earnest, voiceless prayer ;
But ah! my Father knows my love ;
He knows my weakness too,
He knows, and he shall guide us both
In paths we may not rue.

HEARTSEASE.

I have gathered thee, Heartsease, so fragrant and fair,
    Thy name is suggestive of wonderful power,
Were it true, then thy purple and gold I would wear,
    Nor would cast thee aside for one fleeting hour.

It is said, too, that thoughts from thy petals shall spring,
    And I doubt not 'tis truth, as I look in each face,
Inspiration about thee close seemeth to cling
    That comes from thy beauty, and fragrance and grace.

If the sorrowful yearning and passionate souls,
    Could find in thee peace, when so full of unrest,
Could'st thou *ease* human hearts when thy blossoms unfold,
    There are thousands would wear thee and find them-
      selves blest.

My heart beats responsive to tenderest thoughts,
    O, beautiful Heartsease, all potent thy spell,
Thou calmest the tumult that raged in my soul,
    By prophecy true that you ever foretell.

Of a time when all buds, in the radiant glow   .
    Of the sun that's eternal — in life and in light,—
Shall awaken in fragrance and beauty to blow,
    That have been rudely broken and wounded in life.

And tho' quickly you wither, aye soon do ye fade,
    Pure thoughts from the pansies pass into my soul,
And I feel that a something all deathless is mine,
    As I gaze on the blossoms, white, purple and gold.

Thy blossoms are fading, the germ that's within,
    Bringeth forth other flowers much fairer than these,
As I read the sweet promise of hope that you bring,
    Comprehending the wisdom that nam'd the Heartsease.

A SONG OF THE SOUL.

Somehow, all day long on the soft balmy air,
A song comes to me, from,—I do not know where ;
I find I am list'ning its cadences sweet,
At home, or abroad as I walk on the street ;
It comes I am thinking from realms that are far,
Where spirits are gathered —some far-away star.

I hear the soft rustle of gleaming white wings,
I feel the sweet calm some freed spirit brings,
Like essence of poetry, music and song.
It sing, ah ! it sings sweet and low, yet is strong ;
It whispers a tale in my listening ear,—
A beautiful story I'm longing to hear.

The spirit within understandeth its tone,
And answers the voice that the soft winds have borne ;
They answer and call —are communing with me,—
My spirit imprison'd, the other that's free.
Sometimes though this captive within longs to fly,
Unfurl airy wing and mount up through the sky.

Yes, longs to be free as a bird, as it floats
Through the gold-tinted clouds, while singing sweet notes.
Suppress'd shall it be though this life shall be long ?

And only when free shall it burst into song.
I wait, but not idl'y, the voice that shall sing,
I fold, but not sadly, the free-soaring wing ;

I work while I wait, for the time must soon come,
'Twill be while the roses of earth-life yet bloom ;
This captive within holds the wish of my soul —
The longing unuttered so shy, yet so bold,
The spirit revealing, with voice low and sweet,
Is telling of victories over defeat.

The spirit that calling, ambition may be,—
I long to express what it promises me,
But soul-speech may never by tongue be express'd,
Tho' sweet is its promise, it still brings unrest.
The time is now coming, already faint gleams
Illumne the sky of my beautiful dreams ;
No laurel of poet may e'er press my brow,
But songs I shall sing that I'm dreaming of now.

THE OUT-GOING SHIPS.

A stately ship, with sails unfurl'd,
    Is passing out to sea,
I've watched her long ; she rounds the point
    And soon is lost to me.

I watch'd her go, how swift her flight,
    That steady seemed and true—
What winds of fate adverse may blow
    From o'er the waters blue.

O, will she gain the distant port,
  Some far-off sunny shore,
Spice-laden isles in southern seas?
  Will she return once more?

The sky is clear, the waves are calm,
  She sailed out with the tide ;
With hope we wait her unknown fate
  From over ocean wide.

I too have sent forth stately ships
  But one came not again,
It was the pride of all my ships,
  I sent out o'er the main.

The sailors sung, " Ahoy ! Ahoy !"
  Upon the morning air,
I heard "ahoy," with strange wild joy
  Waft o'er the bay so fair.

I sent her forth with cargo worth
  The best my life hath known,
My dearest hopes, my faith was there,
  Borne in my ship that's gone.

I gaze far out o'er sun-lit sea,
  Beyond Columbia's bar,
Where breakers lash the foaming tide,
  Where sail'd my barque afar.

Alas ! no more on this same shore,
  My ship may anchor cast ;
At break of day she sail'd away,
  With dreams too bright to last.

Some wrecks are cast upon the shore,
  And some go down at sea ;
Will my barque gain the wish'd-for port,
  Return with wealth to me ?

A COMMON THEME—HOME.

Of all the pleasures earth can give,
  That's told in song or story,
The one that's nearest perfect bliss,
  And fills the soul with glory ;

Is that sweet realm all beautiful,
  Where helpful angels come,
Found in the sanctuary sweet,
  Of quiet, peaceful home.

Our truest friends we find at home,
  When very great our need,
And though but numb'ring two or three,
  Yet these are friends indeed.

These shall not fail us, many will,
  But if at home we meet
The humble angels, peace and love,
  Will life be calm and sweet.

But if one blessing only, mine,
  And all else be denied me,
Give me dear home with two or three
  Brave, true friends beside me.

IMAGINATION.

This wondrous gift of love divine,
 Immortal mind controlling,
Is no delusive, idle dream,
 Like clouds at sunset rolling.

It weaves a spell o'er ev'ry soul,
 An influence past our knowing,
It comes from God, all pure, divine,
 The Father's love bestowing.

Imagination's golden light
 Tints earth, and sky, and river,
Like distant star-shine, gleaming bright,
 It glows and burns forever.

CHRISTMAS ECHOES.

There's a wonderful song in the air to-night,
 A song that an angel sings,
It is loud and clear and thrilleth the heart
 With tiding of glorious things.
There's the sound of rushing of wings to-night,
 There are tidings of peace to men,
While the angels sing of the beautiful light
 Of a star shining o'er Bethlehem.

Yes, a glittering star in the sky to-night,
 Whose glory fills earth and heaven,
Outshines the fair moon with her brilliant crest,
 A herald of life 'tis given.

This star in its glory arose for the race,
 Far shines its light! the bright morning star,
It seemeth to shine through all time and all space,
 All worlds it illumines afar.

O, glorious star! effulgent thy beam,
 Thy splendor shall never grow dim,
We follow afar thy glittering sheen,
 For surely thou leadeth to Him.
The shepherds are watching their flocks to-night,
 A wonderful choir they hear.
They see that white star in the east so bright,
 While music rings loud and near.

The heavens are glowing with radient light,
 While up beyond orient bars,
The heavenly music which rings on the night,
 Now seemeth to come from the stars.
As wise men of old came with gifts, O, king,
 Of frankincense, myrrh and bright gold,
Our gifts to thy altar, dear Lord we bring,
 The treasure most precious we hold.

Pure incense ascends to thy throne upon high,
 The incense of love that's divine,
One bringeth his faith, while another his work,
 As offerings are brought to thy shrine.
One liveth a martyr his whole life long,
 To a principle stern, untrue,
While one with the love that casteth out fear ·
 Finds much in the vinyard to do,

Another, in doubt, simply clings to the cross,
  With scarcely the courage to pray,
Yet the truth surely come to each earnest soul
  Revealing the light and the way.
And still we are offering gifts at thy shrine,
  Of frankincense, spices and gold,
And still ringing out are the sweet Christmas chimes,
  Again is the old story told,

For light of that star shone forth in the world
  Through the ages before Jesus came,
On all sacred things on this earth shown that light—
  No matter what creed or what name.
It has brought to us knowledge of all noble things,
  Since the dawn of creation began,—
Its star-beams of light shall permeate earth
  'Till the last generation of man.

The vibrating notes of immortal life,
  Are tones which we hear in the song,
And the seraphs are hymning the same songs of praise.
  They sung in the ages long gone.
In the depths of the sky the same stars shine,
  That shone in the blue heavens then,
While our hearts are still turning to the same blessed
    shrine,
  Whose light is the life of all men.

Chime on Christmas bells, all ye stars in the sky,
  With flames that are burning so bright,
Are darkness compared to the real morning star,
  Whose rays are the life and the light.

Then come, let us bring here our offerings pure,
  The best that our hearts can e'er bring,
To shrine of the Truth, which shines for all men.
  For Truth alone is our king.

THE MOON AND STAR.

Once when the new moon shone like silver,
  So bright in the West afar,
And seemed to be closely followed
  By one palely glittering star,—

As over my shoulder I saw it,
  I thought of the ominous sign,
And made a good wish for the morrow ;
  How fond was that sweet wish of mine.

Then brighter, but later each evening,
  The fair moon shone over the sea,
While paler and softer the star-light,
  Because it was farther from me.

I thought of the many lights flashing,
  So bright are, because they are near.
The star may be dim, but comstant,
  With flame ever steady and clear.

While bright is the moon's lamp of silver,
  That flashes its radiant beam,
The star is much better to wish by,
  More steady and true does it gleam.

Though wishing is idle and foolish,
  And wishes so seldom come true,
The full moon ne'er finds us much wiser,
  Than when we had wished with the new.

DEDICATION.

[Of Unity Church, 1891.]

Father, in thy presence now
  We have come with hearts aflame
With the love that emanates
  From thy great and holy name.

Let no worldy thoughts intrude,
  But with spirits pure and free,
Like the rosebud kissed by dew,
  May our souls responsive be.

Now the emanations pure,
  By the christ'ning from above,
Gives thy children power divine;
  Fills our souls with peace and love;

As before Thy shrine we bow,
  Every heart casts out all fear,
Knowing well the tender love
  Of our Father now and here.

In no kingdom far away
  Seek we for a heaven pure,
But within our souls shall be
  All of love that shall endure.

In this house we dedicate
  To thy service, we shall find
That the service of our God
  Is the service of mankind.

TRUE BAPTISM.

There came to the Master, in days long past,
Two chosen desciples a favor to ask,
For seats in his kingdom, the loftiest place,
They knew not his was a kingdom of grace.—
    And thought of him as a temporal king.

The Master with pitying eyes looked up,
He knew to the dregs he must drink the cup,
And knowing they sought but an earthly place,
Divine compassion illumned his face.
    And tender his questioning.

He said to them : " Can ye endure
My baptism, coming so soon and sure ? "
Then quickly they answered, impulsive each man :
" We can, dear Lord, we are able, we can."
    And they meet his look with firm resolve.
The dear Lord gazed with sorrowing smile
Into unseen things, nor spake for awhile,
But when he spake in pittying tone,
The list'ning angels must have known
The Master knew he must suffer alone,
    And still'd their harps in heaven's great dome.

Then gently he said to his followers there :
" Yes, much of my baptism ye shall share,
A firey baptism of trial and of pain
Must be your portion, e'er ye shall gain
That spiritual baptism. The Christ in you,
As it doth in me, shall at last subdue.
 And ye your worthiness then shall prove."

We are desciples, the Christ too is ours,
Develops each soul's most spiritual powers,
We learn as did they of that far olden time,
That the kingdom on earth is the kingdom divine.
That life is a baptism of trial of pain,
And only through baptism the kingdom we gain.
But the Holy Spirit that the Father hath given,
Reveals to the soul the kingdom of heaven
Which is ever the kingdom of love.

ASPIRATION.

Our father in heaven,
Thy love evermore —
My soul fills with rapture,
With holiness, power.
I would live in thy presence
And never grow cold,
Ever prove by my life-work
Thy grace in my soul.

Thy love doth encompass
My being around ;
No fears can assail me,
No fortune can frown, —
Come sorrow or blessing,
The heart on thee stayed
With faith for its anchor
Cannot be dismayed.

The portals of heaven
Opened earthward to me,
My faith and my longing
Reach upward to thee ;
Thou leadeth me, Father,
By thy guiding hand
Through valley, o'er mountain,
To thy promised land.

A SONNET.

I've dreamed of a love that was pure and sweet,
A something holy, that I should meet,
    A love that I should not rue ;
I cannot now tell of all I have dreamed,
Nor how beautiful, pure, the vision has seemed,—
    And now has my dream come true ?
The answer I read in your dear, dear, eyes,
While all my soul in a glad surprise,
    Fulfilleth that dream in you.

ADELIA.

'Tis Christmas eve, Adelia,
    The moon is shining bright,
Its glim'ring sheen surrounds me
    And it stirs my soul to-night.
A night long gone, Adelia,
    Comes back to me again,

With sad sweet mem'ries, darling,
  With joy that yet is pain.

I never knew your heart, love,
  Until the seal was set;
I feared to risk my fate, dear,
  My soul but reaps regret;
I read the story, 'Delia,—
  Wherever we may meet,—
Your life is brave and true, dear,
  While mine but knows defeat.

Was I to blame, my darling,—
  For love is ever blind,—
To think your wealth and beauty
  Would part your fate from mine?
You walk through life so queenly,
  You act so well your part,
He dwells with you serenely,—
  But I can claim your heart.

Though love on earth brings anguish,
  It fills high heaven with bliss;
Our souls will meet, Adelia,
  In other realms than this.
The moonlight falls, Adelia,
  The Christmas stars are bright;
The star of peace that's shining,
  Illumnes my soul to-night.

The Christmas tide is flowing,—
  Is flowing full and free;

I'm going, dearest, going,—
  Reach out your hands to me,—
And know that for thy coming
  A ransomed spirit waits,
A little while, my darling,
  We'll meet within the gates.

KNOWLEDGE.

KNOWLEDGE.

[A lecture delivered before the State Teachers' Institute, at Astoria, Oregon, July 11, 1885.]

Knowledge is the freemasonry of a condition where all are equal, and is indicated by a rank of mind which must take precedence to all external rank. The common-place quotation that " knowledge is power," is as great a truth as was ever uttered by wise sage, or learned philosopher ; yet knowledge without wisdom is not always a power for good. While knowledge is the act of knowing the clear and certain perceptions of truth, wisdom is rather the result of and capacity of making due use of knowledge. The poet Cowper makes a nice distinction, when he says : " Knowledge dwells in heads replete with thoughts of other men ; wisdom in minds attentive to their own, knowledge is the material with which wisdom builds, and is proud that he has learned so much, while wisdom is humble that he knows no more."

This convention of a body of teachers is not only to gain new ideas, more accurate knowledge ; but also the wisdom to properly apply it,—for it is the wise use of knowledge more than its possession, that determine its worth. There is a great difference between imparting and absorbing knowledge, for the one is external, the other internal growth. He who simply absorbs it grows from without, only possessing talent to acquire ; while the within original man has genius to impart. The advent of knowledge has ever been a record of trials, tears, heartaches, and often bloodshed, before its establishment and maintenance; for it reaches its final triumph only through suffering, while its practical use is at the sacrifice of ignorance, and this is too often at the sacrifice of innocence. Every improvement, every advancement in civilization, injures some to benefit others. The highway of knowledge is not always strewn with roses. Conquering science in its onward, triumphal march ruthlessly tramples down whatever opposes its progress, whether ignorance or innocence.

Stephen Montague says: "You diffuse knowledge and the world grows brighter, but discontent and poverty replaces ignorance. One generation is sacrificed to the next." History teaches that from the earliest ages to the present it has often taken ten thousand such lives as yours and mine to accomplish one of God's eternal purposes. The only consolation we derive is that sacrifices now will result in future blessings. Our present liberties and blessings came by the martyrdom of past generations. If to the advocates of the knowledge of truth came the actual realization of the suffering of those sacrificed e'er it be established, many times they could not have the courage to conquer, but would consider it mercy to let ignorance reign in her dark dominion.

Macauley teaches that with the advance of liberalism the human race grows everywhere happier and more enlightened. Sir Archibald Allison teaches that liberalism means revolution and anarchy. James Anthony Froude says: "Both these views may be false, each may be sincere, but he unconsciously drops what does not suit his argument

and fuses such facts as go to make his picture effective."
All labor-saving machinery upon its first introduction
throws thousands out of employment. Every invention,
every revolution of the wheels of progression's car of
knowledge, crushes thousands who are ignorant, yet innocent. The civilization of new countries is death to the
native savage races. Yet events wait not for individuals
or races of men. These facts are great mysteries, for our
finite minds cannot comprehend the dark "whys" of
God, so we wait, and waiting, wonder at the strange provi-
dence of "Him whose ways are indeed past finding out."

Owen Meredith says: "Life begins and ends in doubt,"
while another writes, "Doubt is the offspring of knowledge." We know that doubt must overturn simplicity and
lead to investigation of truth. Shakespeare says : "Knowledge is the wing wherewith we fly to heaven," and again,
"Our doubts are traitors, and make us lose the good we oft
might win." There is some truth in this last quotation,
but I believe our fears are the "traitors," and doubts are
sometimes friends that point to truth. Geothe says: "That
is holy which binds many souls together." Therefore knowledge, which is the strongest tie that can bind and bless
society in a great universal brotherhood, is eminently holy,
for increased scientific and religious knowledge develops
the wealth and progress of the soul. and increases a desire
for cultivation. Progress begets progress, for the mind is
full of the desire to project itself forever onward into new
fields of research. As soon as one truth is demonstrated it
searches the unknown, in the expectation of finding another
and greater. Thought cannot be confined, for the soul of
thought travels free as the music of the waves or the light

of the eternal stars. And though custom does conquer this world of matter, it cannot control the greater world of thought, where our true natures exist. And so mankind have learned to exalt fredom of thought. And there is no law to govern this freedom, for law is only to restrain license. Free schools, free speech, free thought, is a nobler freedom than its martyrs ever dreamed. And so old things are passing away, and we are advancing to a new heaven and new earth of thought, of intellectual reign. But an increase of knowledge is but an increase of doubt and perplexity, and he who invokes knowledge from her urn calls forth a power entailing great responsibilities. Yet from early youth we are taught to gain this wonderful power to improve the intellect, which alone is heir of immortality and which is just as immortal now as it will ever become, for the once awakened soul dies not. It passes through psychological changes, but the soul's language knows no word for death — there is no death for that which wills and thinks. Ah! knowledge is powerful, and can pierce the distant heavens and explore much of the realm of mind, yet fails to peer for one moment into that realm which is so far away beyond the stars, yet which is so close about us that the fluttering heart-beat, the tremulous breath we draw is the boundary of that world which spirit alone may enter, and though we have all the knowledge of the past to aid us, we have not the wisdom to truthfully pierce one moment of that future. So why not tone down our arrogance, confess our ignorance and simply say: "I do not know."

But it is the nature of man to question all things, and not only to understand the truth, but to question why it is truth.

Truth is the offspring of knowledge and research, and its birth is through travail and suffering; and it is only as we become familiar with its justice that it secures happiness. We do not always know when and where truth may be found, for, often in the past has truth been wrapped up in the vagaries of a dispised creed, or rejected religion. We find many of the dim utterances of Confucius, Gautama, Zoroaster and Mahomet, and many other religions and philosophies as firmly established in the accepted religions and creeds of the present day, as are the vague if inspired utterances of the Hebrew prophets. Knowledge demands martyrs, and men have suffered martyrdom all ages for its advancement. Oftentimes not so much for truth as for some little narrow sect or creed, the effort put forth, being *to do good according to their peculiar creed.* Yet while many a great heart is ill assorted with a narrow creed, our creeds are generally in harmony with our intellects. Each new creed-maker goes to the Bible and takes what he wants to answer his purpose, if he can find it there, and adds what *he thinks*; and the Bible, well manipulated, will prove any doctrine in this world. So divisions arise. Why, if facts were as plain as some would have us believe, Christ's prayer that all his people might be one, would have been answered long ago, but almost 1900 years since that prayer was uttered finds them still very far apart. O, if we could sweep these little narrow prejudices forever from our souls, and stand forth in the freedom of our God, whoever, whereever, *whatever* he may be—eating without fear the fruits of the tree of knowledge and of life—irrespective of men or creeds; then indeed might wisdom be justified of her works. When knowledge divests theology of some of its inconsis-

tencies, then shall we be able to understand and see clearly
the germ of truth that lies within. Truth, like a kernel of
wheat, occupies but a small space in the universe, but
there are more possibilities of bread for earth's hungering
thousands in it than in all the chaff in the world. One
germ of truth has more salvation in it than all the theology
this side of the grave,—and there will be no theology the
other side. And so we think and doubt, and perhaps lose
much faith, for earnest thought is often the death-blow to
unquestioning faith ; for, upon investigation we are obliged
to overturn much that we have accepted as knowledge, but
which wisdom dare not apply, or, some of our accepted
theology. Truth demands the sacrifice of one. Which
shall it be? While we do not need a new religion, we do
need a great reformation of the old, just as our school-
books, maps and charts need revising once in a while to
meet the demands of the age. Ah! we do not know what
realms awakened thought leads to, for the shadows of
mystery and the bright gleams of light chase each other
ever. While there is always an unsolved mystery just
ahead of us, there is a light follows to dispel the gloom, but
the brighter the dispelling light the more clearly it enables
us to discern a greater mistery just beyond us still. It is
just as absurd to ask a man to be entertained by a primer
all his days as to ask him to cling to old beliefs after he has
outgrown them. There is some truth in all creeds, but all
of truth in none.

James Anthony Froude says: "It is certain that com-
monwealths, institutions, creeds, are mortal as we ourselves;
that they must pass through the same stages of youth,
maturity, corruption and death as each of us pass

through. It may be that the future may be like the
past and that to everything that has an organized existence
there is an appointed growth, decline and end. If theology
was rid of the rubbish of superstition and prejudice which
envelops it there would be but a small grain left. For our
theology is founded on pagan mythology. We do not do
away with their gods, we only substitute our idea of God
in place of theirs. Yet our ideal of God is much higher,
purer and better than theirs, but future generations will
come much nearer his real attributes than have we, for we
have not all of knowledge yet. While firmly believing in
a God of purity, justice and mercy, we may claim it as our
right to doubt much of the teachings of men respecting
him. It is not best for us to brand as infidels or skeptics
those who, believing in a God of goodness and wisdom,
yet, who are honest enough to stand up in the face of opposition and honestly declare I do not understand him. There
are mysteries which will be mysteries still, even though
this intellect. this immortality within us, progress to the
knowledge of gods. The best part of all or any religon, that,
simmered down, teaches a pure and noble life is salvation
and security. Man, by his divisions of the sheep from the
goats, makes many mistakes, but he who is perfect in wisdom makes none, and even though we be surprised at his
divisions they are just, for the critics up there are just and
thoroughly understand humanity. So in wise beliefs we
need fear no evil, and even though we err, we need not so
much dread justice as hope for mercy. There are many
ruined temples · still standing whose gods and creeds
crumbled into dust ages ago. So some men stand to-day,
silent empty temples, representing a vanished delusion, or

are floating along in their little ark of salvation, with all
the rest of the world drowning outside. The human heart
is full of strange delusions, but the greatest are the creeds
representing its beliefs and prejudices.

The seeds of knowledge may slumber long before the
fruits of wisdom ripen in the soul, yet the germ of life may
be there. Kernels of wheat have been found in ancient
tombs where the germ had kept the secret of life hidden
well through the long centuries. And there is a beautiful
legend of the seed of the heliotrope being found in the hand
of a mummy, which upon being planted sprung forth into
fragrance and beauty after thousands of years ; waiting the
time and opportunity, in the far future, when for unborn
generations it should at last blossom in rare perfection and
diffuse its wonderous perfume. So may the germ of truth
be held back for ages in the vice-like grip of some grim
skeleton hand of a dead, yet embalmed doctrine, before the
knowledge of its fragrance and beauty is shed forth for
mankind.

There may be nothing new under the sun, and you teachers
may not be discoverers of new realms, unless the mind of
childhood reveal it unto you ; but you may be successful
in the faculty of imparting the discoveries of the knowledge
of others, and he who arouses in the mind of the child the
longing after the attainment of knowledge, comes as near
as man can come to the creative attributes of God.

He who imparts an intelligent apprehension, gives a better understanding of the living languages all around us as
they are, a knowledge that meets the wants and incidents
of daily life, is a more desirable teacher than he who

spends so much time on the uncertain history of the past, or the dead languages of an accomplished era. There are those who seem to possess the faculty of showing off a child' signorance much more than bringing out, or increasing his knowledge. The teacher is the moral and mental whetstone, on which the child sharpens his wits, therefore it becomes necessary that between the disciplined mind of the teacher, and the untutored mind of the child, there should be a bond of sympathy. Love, the central emotion, around which all other emotions revolve, and from which all nobler emotions evolve, is the bridge which spans the chasm between the intelligence of the teacher and the ignorance of the child. The educated, cultivated mind transmits knowledge, and heart reacts upon heart, and mind upon mind; the simple, childish mind draws upon the intellectuality of the stronger and imparts freshness and originality to that which is in danger of becoming merely booky.

The most successful teacher has not, necessarily, the greatest amount of knowledge, but the wisdom to properly apply well what he does understand. In instructing and benefiting others, it becomes necessary that we stop to consider, and realize, if we can, the probable difference between the fiber of individual souls, or our own soul, from the multitude of those around us.

One of the most beneficent gifts bestowed upon humanity is adaptibility. Unless one have adaptability and can gracefully conform to surrounding circumstances, knowledge may as often prove a detriment as a blessing. Yet to possess adaptibility one must have quick perceptions and readily read human nature. The teacher of the young has for study before him volume first, of the wonderful book of humanity, a sort of primer, whose pages, seemingly so simple, are sometimes written in strange characters, difficult to understand and translate. Perhaps the child is more like the mental arithmetic, which is full of difficult problems; but the mental arithmetic, thoroughly understood, furnishes the key to the higher mathematics, and the primer is but the prelude to all that follows in the great field of literature. So the mind of childhood, appreciated and understood, furnishes the key to all the more intricate phases of youth, manhood and age that follow, and he who understands children holds the golden key that unlocks the great heart of humanity. Christ taught that inasmuch as ye help the least of these "ye have done it unto me."

In my short-sighted, human way (and that is all the way we have of looking at things), I have often wondered what condition we, as a race, would have been in if Eve had not eaten of the forbidden fruit of the tree of knowledge. According to a literal rendering of the story of the Garden of Eden, God's original intention was that the race of mankind should be without knowledge, although he planted the tree of knowledge of *good* and *evil* in the midst of that beautiful garden, whose beauties the inhabitants without knowledge could not appreciate or understand. Here spread before them in perfection, was nature with her wonderful lessons to man untranslatable, without one ray of knowledge to lighten the darkness of his ignorance. Man in this state was innocent, not from any good or evil in his nature, but because like the infant he knew no wrong. Paradise was a garden of innocence, because of ignorance.

But the serpent, wisdom, bade Eve taste the tempting fruit of the tree of knowledge. With the ancients the serpent was symbolical of wisdom, and also indicated subtlety. Wisdom charms us still, and by its subtlety knowledge plans and works. The Great Teacher when sending his disciples forth to teach, admonishes them to be wise and gentle, in the remarkable words : " Be ye wise as serpents and harm- less as doves." Did you, whose profession it is to instill knowledge, ever think that, reasoning from a literal inter- pretation of the scriptures, it was by the evil one know- ledge became the heritage of our race, and that you are laboring to advance his work ? Strange paradox, is it not, that to you 'tis given to put the forbidden fruit to the lips of innocent youth ? According to this literal interpreta- tion again, God placed the knowledge of *evil*, before our first parents, commanding them not to eat, for fear they become as gods; and if he had not countermanded his own order, or the evil one persuaded Eve to disobey, we, her offspring, would have had no ray of knowledge ; but by our first mother's disobedience and fearful sacrifice, the possibility of attaining knowledge became a heritage of our race. A grand and noble heritage, no matter who made it possible. She, by eating, invoked knowledge which is at once an angel of light and demon of evil, for the fruit was of *good and evil*, two great forces which, in turn, rule the destiny of the world. Ah ! how eagerly we, her de- scendants, eat the fruit of that awful tree of knowledge and of life, which from the beginning has tempted all mankind, and though it often leaves a bitter taste, yet we long to eat and *live*.

How fair to our first parents must have appeared Eden, when a knowledge of its wonders and possibilities burst in upon their ignorance, when they were leaving it forever! How often in all the ages since then have their descendants awakened to the realities of paradise, only to behold its glories fade away like dying colors from beautiful dreams! And, just as they realize it is Eden, adverse fate bids them wander forth, where too often thorns and thistles curse the ground. But though exiled from that Eden of beauty, have we not gained the far more desirable Eden of possibilities to aspiring genius, that that taste made possible to man? It is through travail and anguish of soul that knowledge was born, as were Eve's children; yet is it not better to have lost an Eden of ignorance and gained an Eden of knowledge? For the loss of that paradise made the nobler Eden possible. Then, better knowledge and anguish than paradise and ignorance.

Though the original tree of knowledge was planted in Eden, it has taken root in every land, and its seeds find all soils congenial, springing up in light and beauty, dispelling mystery after mystery, growing fairer and more beautiful than when in Eden. And, though we are sometimes intimidated by the flaming sword of ignorance, which would keep us from gathering its precious fruits, yet we may eat and live. I believe with Swedenborg that the whole story of the Garden of Eden is a beautiful allegory, and nothing more, and if we thus believe and give it a spiritual interpretation, obstacles will be removed and we may feel the force of its illustrations, and lose none of its beauties or truths. Study and thought brings form out of the chaos and confusion of ideas. What poetry in the idea of comparing knowledge to a tree which branches out in all directions, with its branches crowned with leaves, flowers and fruits, which, as the ages roll on, beneath suns, storms and calms increase in size, beauty and strength. Wisdom assures us if we eat we shall *not* surely die, but progress to immortal life. Ah! there are so many things which we cannot prove to be so, yet which we do not believe or understand! There is nothing in all the realm of animal life that comes into life as destitute of knowledge as man, and nothing can compare with him in the possibilities of attainment. In this life, by knowledge, he may become the demi-god, and what development may crown progression in the life that continues beyond the grave, "hath not entered into the heart of man."

If Plato's doctrine of Anemnesis were true, and our knowledge is but the reminiscence of ideas contracted in another and prior existence, there would be no need of teachers, for we would gradually remember all that is apportioned for us to know, without effort on our part. While this is not the accepted doctrine, we sometimes witness such seeming proofs of intuitive knowledge that we are almost startled out of our established belief. For things do often come to us by intuition, and although intuition is not knowledge, we often mistake it for it. Intuition is an understanding of something without effort on our part, or the part of others to enlighten us. Whence comes it? We often arrive at truth without any previous preparation of knowledge that leads up to it. This intuitive knowledge comes to us at times, opening glimpses of that life that lies beyond ; a something truer, yet less tangible, a

destiny to which we are inevitably hastening, which is our
abiding place; a something which theology, which is full
of glaring contradictions, does not reach or teach, and the
knowledge of which we have not yet attained, but which the
soul does understand; and by which it somehow comprehends
that eternity, with all its vastness, and immortality is ours.
This is why the problem of futurity occupies the most of
the best thought of mankind. This knowledge hangs over
a wise man as some brilliant sunset cloud hangs in splendor
over a high mountain peak with the sun shining through
it. It is a cloud, yet of glory, not of darkness, which
speaks of more than visible beauty. It unfolds beatific
visions that exalt the soul to a state that is above, and more
than place. What intuition is to man, instinct is to animals.
Even the lower orders of mankind have instinctive or intuitive knowledge to perceive atmospheric changes and phen-
omena—the power to understand the voices of beasts and
birds—instinctively reading in nature what science reveals
in his more intellectual brother. This offers a strange vista
to speculative reverie. Knowledge is a mighty rock in a
weary land; and to teachers 'tis permitted to smite this
rock, and from it gush fountains of living waters which
form rivers of wisdom, flowing to the uttermost parts of the
earth, carrying immortal life to the souls of men.

The river of science flows in a deep, straight course,
searching out the hidden mysteries and demonstrating facts,
while truth builds her defenses on its shores, and art rears
fair palaces and calmly enjoys the result of labor and research. History, with its broad stream, bringing knowledge down through the vanquished centuries, revealing
many lost arts which avail us much in these later days.

Mysteries which magicians have left behind them—secrets for ages undusted—that we may read the records of the past. Experience builds citadels upon these heights. Flowing parallel to history is the stream of politics. Its crimson billows cast wrecks upon the strand, and the moaning waves strangely blend the tones of grand, martial music with the discord of despair and disappointment, for it is a treacherous tide. Along its winding shores war builds her forts, and there are fields of carnage and of blood and the dark fortress of envy, from which fly the poisoned shafts of malice, falsehood and revenge; and there are many graves in which lie ambition, glory and renown, with all their brilliant dreams. Opposite to this, from the rock, of knowledge, gush the sweet fountains of poetry and music, singing on their way through fair secluded dells, where there are moss-crowned rocks, clinging vines, fragrant flowers, and ferns, and singing birds. In their shining waves of light are mirrored the azure sky, golden sunshine and fleecy clouds; while youth, beauty, laughter and joy stray along the verdant shores, keeping time to the music of the merry spray and weaving garlands to crown their radient brows. There is one deep, turbid stream, the greatest of them all. The river of theology, whose dark waves have engulfed much of the best and ablest thought of the minds of men. Upon its shores strong fortresses are built; they are prisons and madhouses and their inmates have been sages, philosophers and priests—men of knowledge, yet lacking in wisdom. Theology is a wierd and tortuous stream, and though sometimes flowing parallel to the river of wisdom, it is at last lost in the wild mad sea of speculation and of doubt; beneath whose seething waters

many a fair bark is sunk which stranded on the rocks of
doctrine and debate. Not far from this flows a deep stream,
calm, clear and beautiful. Majestically it sweeps through
stately forests, extending plains and lofty mountains; and
the fair cities of science, temperance and truth, are built
upon its shore. It is fed by the everliving fountains of
honor, morality, justice, mercy and divine love. The
music of its waves send forth hymns of *true* patrotism, love
of country and of home; and the sweet songs of faith and
immortality float upward upon strong white wings, bearing
the soul away on pure melody above *this* world of longing
and of hope, until it rises to meet *that* world of glory and
fulfillment. Upon these shores faith, hope and security have
reared their white temples, which shall ever represent a
living religion which has but three words for its creed :
Love, Justice, Immortality. This is the river of wisdom,
and flows into the great ocean of eternal peace.

Teachers, these are the streams flowing from the rock of
knowledge, whose fountains you unseal. "Blessed are
ye that sow beside *all* waters." Out there you hear the
ocean waves moaning, surging, thundering forevermore.
You cannot stay the rushing tides that come and go—ebb
and flow until time shall be no more ; nor the great river of
the west, the mighty Columbia, pouring her floods into that
vast, boundless sea ; so shall knowledge pour her deep, ex-
haustless stream into futurity, and all the combined forces
of opposition, ignorance and fear shall have no power to
stay the onward rushing, overwhelming flood. Wafted
back to us from the unexplored shores across that sea—
softly whispering through the rose-marine spirit of the
mist—intuitive knowledge reveals the throne of eternal

wisdom, from which flows the pure river of life, on whose bright shores grow the trees of knowledge and of life immortal, which bear no fruit of sin, but whose leaves are for the healing of *all the nations.*

ONLY A BABY.

ONLY A BABY.

Dead! Only a baby, a little wee baby — not much loss to this great world with its teeming millions. Nothing, did you say? Ah, what a world of hopes, fears and possibilities clustered around its frail life.

To the young mother who, with streaming eyes and heaving breast, looks for the last time upon that beautiful, delicate flower, it is much. O God! it is everything — the ruthless sundering of the dearest ties of earth. Pain is said to be the deepest, most real thing in our natures. The strongest links between mother and child is the union of keenest physical pain and tenderest love; consequently when death takes the little one, 'tis the mother who feels the keenest anguish. Death cuts short an infinity of possibilities, when he breaks the fragile bud from the parent stem.

Only a baby; yet what untold probabilities of suffering, of sacrifice, of sin, of goodness, of all the emotions of life that wear the heart out with conflicts, has it escaped. To those who live the allotted time on earth, the crown of true nobility is gained only by conflict, yet this frail one has "gained the crown without the conflict."

Only a baby; an immortal soul awakened out of the vast eternity of silence, to sleep never more, but go on, and on, through the great eternity of blessedness.

This busy world pauses not when its greatest geniuses,

its most illustrious sons and daughters leave it, and there is not even one little ripple outside of a very few hearts, when "only a baby," the merest speck of humanity — a passing breath of immortality hovering for such a little time between the "two eternities," drops out into the boundless, fathomless sea. But the delicate, snowy bud, with all its possibilities of wondrous beauty and fragrance, is transplanted to the Paradise of God. And though you shall miss the affection, the little cunning ways, and all that promised to pervade the atmosphere of home, like the perfume of a lovely rose, yet up there she is nourished by the waters of life, and the fruit of the Tree of Life. Thy little one is like a fragile flower in a golden vase, watered by the everlasting fountains of divine love.

Though this lesson of faith may be learned through bitter anguish, yet in his own good time the Father's loving purpose shall be revealed to thee. As the iron anchor sinks through slime and mud far below the surface and holds the stately ship secure upon the tempestuous waves above, so let the anchor faith sinks through wretchedness and despair into the soul, holding it safe, and even though the day is dark and the hour bitter, God's light will break through the clouds and tears, and illumine the trusting heart with undying rays of peace and blessedness. So we brush aside the dew of tears and welcome the sunlight of faith, even the little shining ray that "only a baby" leaves on its passage to the skies. As we mourn over these incompleted lives we wonder why (since they but seem shatter our hopes) they were sent; but if our eyes be but touched by the divine light, we may see how these unfinished lives were interwoven into, and influence our own, so differently, yet, with purer influence than if they had fulfilled the allotted earthly years, for lives are not numbered by years, but by influence, and the guidance of "only a baby" in the spirit realm may lead us in straighter ways, more peaceful paths, than it would if left to walk earth's ways and experience its temptations. For that life entering there, yet remembered here, will be like a star whose light emanates from that world and irradiates this, leading and guiding us to those many mansions, all beautiful, in the city of our God, where the doors open outward for all God's children, from whence they may descend to us, and where we too may enter in and dwell with them.

Thank God the door of human faith opens toward heaven, the door of divine love opens toward earth. So that our human faith and longing meets divine love and fulfillment; and to the trusting heart may come, God's "peace that passeth understanding" and the soul be made strong and brave.

THOUGHTS

UPON

THE ÆSTHETIC;

AN ADDRESS

Delivered before the Musical Alumni, Willamette
University, June 9, 1887.

BY MRS. OLIVE S. ENGLAND.

SALEM, OREGON :

E. M. WAITE, STEAM PRINTER AND BOOKBINDER.

1887.

THOUGHTS .

UPON

THE ÆSTHETIC;

AN ADDRESS

Delivered before the Musical Alumni, Willamette
University, June 9, 1887.

By Mrs. Olive S. England.

SALEM, OREGON :
E. M. WAITE, STEAM PRINTER AND BOOKBINDER.
1887.

ᏀHE ADDRESS.

...

The æsthetic really means *all* that reaches and contributes to the higher life of man through the sensibilities and emotions rather than the intellectual faculties. Progressive civilization may be guaged by the degree of attention paid to objects of refined beauty and pure elevating loveliness. A noted historian said that "The history of arts and sciences is the history of the powers of the human mind, and their inventors have labored for all ages of the world, have provided at a great distance for all our occasions." He placed music sixth in the ratio of importance. That it should rank as one of the most important and best means of intellectual development, none deny. It is a very ancient study. Its history, like that of other arts, sciences and religions being lost in ancient mythologies.

Some authorities claim that man first learned music from warbling birds. All authorities agree that the first musical instrument was the shell of a tortoise. Mythology tells us this was made into a musical instrument by the infant Hermes, who, when but four hours old took a walk and seeing a tortoise said, "Thou slowly crawlest, now there is no use in thee, thou shalt die and sing forever." So he killed it and across the shell he stretched strings made of oxhide, thus making the first lyre. This he gave to Apollo saying, "To those who touch it not knowing how to draw forth its speech it will babble strange nonsense and rave with uncertain moanings, but thy knowledge is born with thee and my lyre becomes thine." At the touch of Apollo's hand, waves of such sweet sounds rolled forth that the trees bent to listen. Pythagoras taught that the world was formed by harmony of sound. He annexed certain peculiar sounds to the rolling spheres, and one rule laid down for his disciples was to adore the whispering wind. He also taught that the distance of the celestial spheres from the earth corresponds to the proportion of notes in a musical scale. He and Plato both believed "everything musical of divine origin ;" that God gave us this corrective of soul and body so that our powers and impulses should be harmonized into mutual assistance and perfect unison. Pythagoras made use of music to tranquilize his mind, and it was the custom of his disciples when rising from bed to awaken the mind with music in order to render them more fit for the duties of the day, and also before retiring for the night to calm their thoughts before they slept. How poetic the thought of being lulled to dreams and rest, and awakened to duty by sweet melodies which softens and throws a charm over the stern realities of life, and tranquilizes the mind for the reception of truth. On account of the wisdom and temperance of Pythagoras, his disciples called him the son of God, (though this was about 600 years before Christ's time) they said he was the only mortal by the gods allowed to hear the "music of the spheres." Whether or not this was true he must have heard divine notes of truth for he surely possessed the true idea of the solar system, which, afterwards revived by Copernicus, was established by Newton, and many in the world to-day are beginning to accept his idea of God. In the language of another I would ask, "Who, acquainted with the laws of sound can positively declare that this was impossible, for Pythagoras with swelling soul to catch the harmoniously blended notes produced by the planets plunging through space. Is it not scientifically demonstrated that there is in the movement of soundwaves a maximum and minimum limit above and below which the mortal ear ceases to receive vibrations? Then what a universe of harmonies unknown to human sensibilities, and philosophies may be filling all the circling spheres with melodies." We know there are certain states or conditions when mortal ears may literally hear—it may be the music of the spheres. Often when death is near and the spirit is just leaving its earthly house, doth the ears by some occult process by us not understood—attuned to higher and holier melodies, catch heavenly tones of other worlds than ours, even while the lips have power to tell of its seraphic harmonies.

It is said that the number of really great musicians is small in comparison with the greatness of men in other vocations. One reason may be, because of the infinite painstaking and constant practice required to keep up to any standard of excellence, for it is an exacting tyrant with all its allurements, and though possessing the greatest and most agreeable influence, with the exception of oratory, over the emotions, is the most fleeting of all accomplishments and its influence more unsubstantial than a dream, there is nothing to fix its modulations, nothing remains to attest its charms and quality, *nothing!* And we arouse from its spell vaguely wondering what power bewitched us. Yet its sweet tones are not lost, and though fleeting, each time 'tis heard it leaves the soul of a better, different quality than it was before this sense of grandeur pervaded it. It awakens in the spiritual nature the chords already there belonging to the soul, and all that benefits and betters it will work continually in ever new and grander ways, strengthening, refining and advancing it. Music is the only passion sure of being gratified in heaven. In other branches supreme excellence appeals directly to our appreciation, but the nearer perfection music attains the more cultivation is required to appreciate its beauties. Of all the arts and science anciently, music was most generally cultivated. It was used at their solemn sacrifices, festivals, and even at their meals. The Jews uttered their prophesies in song until prophesy came to mean song, and to a great extent the music of a nation is its prophesy. The world has been prone to take up the Jewish hymns, poems and songs, and build a religious theory out of them. In our interpretation of these we do them and ourselves injustice. Supposing two or three thousand years hence our songs were as literally interpreted as are theirs, think what a fearful jumble we would be in to literally interpret our contemporary poets. We have our minstrel songs, (and they are suited to those who sing them) our ballads, hymns, war and salvation army songs. Supposing future generations would collect these into a book and use them for the foundation of a theological system, and ostracise those who did not receive them as truth. It is to be hoped that in future centuries they will not be placed as a rule of life in the hands of a people ignorant of their true significance. For in trying to follow them and their future expounders they will be divided into more sects than are the followers of the Jewish psalms now, and our enlightenment is considered superior to theirs. Let these hymns, poems and psalms represent their original significance and there is inspiration in them, but place them entirely beyond their possible meanings, and there is anything *but* inspiration in them.

Music may very properly be divided into the scientific and emotional. The scientific may be subdivided into head, hand and heel music. Some who make complete success of mechanical or theoretical music are not endowed with the deep feeling and fine imagination to be the true interpreters of ideal music, that which awakens and controls the emotional and spiritual qualities. Head music consists of theory, and is certainly intellectual. While one may be an acknowledged success in this, and it is eminently necessary, yet, if music consists more of agreeable tones than deep theories or fine execution, he is *not* a success. To become a fine hand musician (for one may be this without theory) requires but an ordinary mind, robust health to endure the mechanical drill and skillful fingers. There is also great facination in that quality of music which seems to lend wings to the heels, and one may succeed in *this* without much brain capacity. In fact, lightness of head is apt to promote lightness of heels. This branch may cultivate grace of motion and some society success, yet not be much of a cultivator of either physical or intellectual power. Still there is much to admire in head, hand and heel music, especially when the art is so consumate as to conceal all trace of effort. But heart, or emotional music must be deeper than the finger-tips, above, beyond all theory, and of that character to which the halt, the lame can respond, for it strikes responsive chords on that complex, yet finely strung instrument, the human heart, and it is not always the whitest, best trained fingers that bring forth its sweetest tones. The heart is very sensitive to the influence of the musician and quick to discern the true from the false, which consists not so much in *skill* as intensity of feeling, to which magic spell our souls respond, while we have only an intellectual admiration for the merely scientific. Doubtless the scientific is as true as the inspirational, and we claim not the superiority of one over the other, but they are different gifts. Isms and theories fail to sound the depths of the heart, for it must be sounded by the emotions, and it is the peculiarity of musical influence that it is emotional, having but little in common with the practical. Not that we should cultivate the emotional to the exclusion of the practical, for practical experiences are ours every day, and we must be familiar with their meanings, but there are but few who are expounders and interpreters of the emotions. This perceptive music partakes of the nature of religion, and if not religion, is surely a great leap toward it, for both music and religion are closely allied branches of the science of the soul, and through inspiration music *intuitively* imparts the knowledge that science *demonstrates* and ennobles us, and each ennobling impression we receive, from *whatever* source, is a shining link in immortal inspiration. Inspiration sustains the same relation to music as a science as the soul does to the body. While the science of harmony is the perfect arrangement of music, the melody is the soul running all through it, and we enjoy it according to the mood we are in, yet it often changes the mood. If we understood the substance and structure of our souls we might be able to account for the strange emotions, moods and inconsistencies which take possession of them. Music awakens *all* the faculties, the most stirring powers of the heart are exerted at its wondrous bidding, causing the dancer to keep step, arousing the warrior to go bravely forth to battle, and teaching religion to sing anthems of praise and adoration. We concede that in many ways it has not the greatness and splendor of oratory, for nothing will exceed eloquence for lasting impressions, nor the immortality of architecture and sculpture, the beauty of painting, nor the practical truth of science. Yet its claims to greatness consists in wider and more varied influence. There are musical tones everywhere. Even in nature's work-a-day world. The shining brook, pearly cascade and rushing waterfall, are ever waltzing, whirling and dancing to their own music. Nature's grander, deeper chords are struck by the thunder-tones, whose deep bass voices sounding from heaven to earth, from earth to heaven, cause no wonder that ignorance and superstition have believed such tones proclaimed God's wrath. Or, in the mysterious waves that bring their messages from sea to land, and carries the answer from land to sea on the flowing and ebbing tides. But we hear the softer, gentler tones in the whispering breeze, the song of birds, the

Æolian harp, the laughter of a child. Every tone of the human
voice, every sound of Nature moves to the harmony of musical vibrations, touching some string of the harps of God. The immortal
soul has its divine harmonies unheard by mortal ears, for music is
indeed an invisible angel who cannot be clasped with material
hands, but whose shining drapery is illusive as azure clouds of
sunlight.

There is that in *all* æsthetic branches which eludes methods and
theories, and only reaches or is reached by intuition. While all the
arts, sciences and philosophies in their varied and beautiful forms
exalt the spirit, yet it is through the medium of sound that Nature
more directly appeals to the deeper emotional qualities. And the
climax of spiritual exaltation is reached quickest and surest
through music, oratory and poetry. Sound and sight are the
greatest of the five senses, and sound is greater than sight, not for
practical, physical purposes certainly, but for eternal spiritual cultivation. What the ear hears is in its influence like the perfume of
the flower, sending the elixir of life through and exalting the sensibilities by a more subtle sense than the eye possesses. The
æsthetic may be divided into two groups of threes. Those which
cultivate and appeal to the soul by sight, and those which influence by sound. Each group forms a perfect and separate chord,
and yet any tone of either chord blends into perfect harmony with
all the others. First, we shall consider those of sight, which are
sculpture, architecture and painting. These form a grand chord,
and are for outward adorning, so the eye reveals them to the soul.
Exterior things do indeed dignify and adorn us, but the interior
things which make of us angel or demon.

Those which are for the inward furnishing, and whose meaning
is conveyed to the spirit by sound, or by the ear, are oratory, poetry
and music. These are three of the grandest tones in the universe,
and are exceeded by but one soul sense, and that is intuition, and
through the perceptives *when they partake of inspiration* these become *intuition* and *intuition* is God. This is not mere sentiment.
It is truth, and one of the most important though least understood
of all truths. These two grand chords acts as foils, brightening and

not diminishing one the luster and glory of the other. The one is art, the other is nature. Each tone of these chords like stars differ only in glory, deriving their light from the same source and sending it out on the same great mission of intellectual light and heavenly beauty. To say that a mysterious sympathy pervades and unites them is to say no new things. Neither do we understand why, or *what* it is. Yet if a person excel in one of these in the emotional sense, he has, if not great talent, at least taste for all. To the true painter the spirits of architecture and sculpture calls. To the heart musician the spirit of poetry and oratory sing beautiful songs—they commune together. Having genius for the æsthetic is to be possessed of a living impetuosity, a beautiful disorder of thought which infinitely transcends the regularities of logic or studied art. As its expression gushes forth from the pent up fountains of song, it reveals originality, excites the imagination, soothing the passions into pure and deep emotions, or, all combined, speak by the outpourings of either, while *all* answer that high behest of the infinite, and are the audible voices of invisible things, in which God speaks in the language of emotions, which are the rounds of the ladder of thought, by which we ascend to Him and his angels descend to us. Some spirits live in the clouds and are filled with dreams; they do not descend to the earthly, yet more solid footing of hill, mountain, rock, wood and stream. Well, the gold-tinted clouds, far azure-fields of ether, are for the light and airy wings of imagination—and *spirit* must *soar ;* but we are possessed of two natures, and though the spirit deal with the invisible, the physical must descend to the practical. Yet *both are actual ;* but both are *not* tangible. The tangible is the mortal, dying, represented by things *seen ;* but things *heard* are of the same substance as thought or inspiration, and are part of the ever-living soul, changing, progressing forever, causing the doors of the soul to open and the sweet angels, poetry and song enter in. These voices of Nature must speak. They awaken new hopes and arouse old memories, and we discern the Divine language in its elements, for of such is the Great Eternal Soul. Herein lies the difference between the mechanical and inspired. You and I have felt the power of inspiration, for it is a grander, nobler quality now than

ever before. It speaks in the language that Nature instills in
hearts, and increases in proportion to intellectual development and
appreciation, or, in proportion to the *world's great need of it.*
There are singers whose voices carry the force of inspiration, who
may not have the power of lungs and vocal organs, for lungs and
vocal organs are far from constituting the music of the soul ; and
there is a wide difference between the forceful expression of nature
and that affectation which art vainly attempts to supply. Yet, art
is very capable of polishing the diamond that Nature makes.
Some degree of excellence may be attained by application in all
æsthetic branches except poetry and emotional music. The poet
and inspired musician must be *born* with soul full charged with its
great commission, and its expressions be yours or mine by divine
inheritance. Even that successful talent, determination, fails to
raise one much above the common place unless he bring from that
vague eternity from which we come that mysterious power which
arouses the heart to contemplation of that eternity to which we go.
We have reliefs, paintings, statutes of the ancients with which we
may compare our own, and the history of music, yet not one tone
of its sweet voices has floated down over the centuries for us to
judge its merits by. We have the living, breathing principle in-
tensified. It leaves the instrument of which it was the soul, as the
soul leaves the body of which it was the immortal spark. The instrument is destructible, but the sweet tones which pervaded it are
immortal life. What more fleeting than sound 'tis an unseen thing
like the spirit of life, but by the emotions 'tis appropriated and
contributes to the concord of the soul and lives, undying harmony.

Human sympathy is born of sorrow, but is the sweetest note ever
sounded, and produces unison of hearts. After the recent terrible
mine explosion at Naniomo, the horrible discord of disaster, death
and ruin which struck we know not why, was quickly followed by
the tender responsive chord of God-like love and sympathy which
also passeth understanding, as human love responds from all over
the land with aid and blessing. There are times when discords of
evil and crime like those of a Kissane, or the incendiary who set
fire to that palace of wondrous architecture and beauty, Hotel del
Monte, causes our faith in humanity to waver; but we find it

blessed not to hear these discords by listening to sweeter strains that tell of heroes such as Hutson who descended into the fearful hell-pit of the mine to literally " rescue the perishing" until he lost his life for his fellow men. I know not his creed. I do not think any questions were asked at heavens portal. The lowly Nazarene is there—he knows his own. And though this man may have made no music on earth sweeter than the creaking machinery that lowered him into that chasm of fire and darkness, and though he bore no other token than the black crown of deadly gas he wore about his brow with which the demon of that pit had crowned him—yet crown more glorious could not be worn, for the blackness of the coal has turned to diamonds there. The only crown we will ever wear must be of *earth, earthy;* and he who sings the "music of heaven" must practice it here, for the golden harps won't seem so awkward in our hands if we take a few lessons on the human harps. Angel harpstrings may be swept by hands that are rough and red, but what helpfulness in the hand that opens in ministra-tions of love, reaching out to lead "beside the still waters" the weak and despondent, putting the harp of hope into feeble, tired hands, raising the fallen angels of earth into light and life *here* and *now.* Such hands may not be skillful on ordinary musical in-struments, but they lovingly touch the chords of thoughtful ten-derness and fill *this* world with notes of song. Such hands *never* loosen their clasp on the Eternal. Ah ! well, the world is awaken-ing to nobler ideas of angel harps and crowns, and the 19th century angels are laying aside the old cracked instruments of praise, and are beginning to sing the dear *old* songs in *new* keys better under-stood for the *new heaven* and *new* earth of a more rational under-standing and better appreciation *of our God.* Humanity is set together like different parts of song or the music of a chorus. Some natures supply the sweet melody, some the deep toned strength of bass, others the intermediate alto and tenor, while *some* are the keynotes of the age in which they live. Washington, Lin-coln, Harriet Beecher Stowe, and even old John Brown struck the keynotes of physical freedom, as Luther, Sweedenborg, Channing and others have struck the higher tones of mental freedom from religious thralldom. Homer, Shakspeare, Milton, Burns, Byron, touched the wild, impetuous key tones in poetry and song. Hume, Gibbon, Rollins, Macauley, the deep toned chords of history. Plato, Socrates, Pythagoras, Franklin, Newton, Darwin, Edison, have sounded true notes of philosophy and science. Alexander, Hannibal, Napoleon, Grant, the harsher tones of war. Demosthenes, Alcibiades, Ingersol, Wendell Phillips and Beecher aroused the enthusiasm of oratory and eloquence. Phidias, Praxiteles, Raphael, Michael Angelo, Titian and Turner have shown us the beautiful in art. Mozart, Jennie Lind, Bethoven, Patti, Wagner, awakened music's witching spell, while Zoroyaster, Guatama, Confucious, Keshab, Chunder Sen, Jesus of Nazareth, struck the terrible, the true, the tender, plaintive and pathetic in religion and reform. For religion and reform *ever* prove the truth of the words of Jesus, I come to bring a sword, but my peace I leave with you. These and many, many others have struck the keynotes, and given character to the greatest principles of life. The heroes and inventors of arts, and expounders of science and philosophy are quite as worthy of admiration and reverence as are the heroes of blood and battles. They, *too*, have had their moral and mental battle-fields covered with slain, fears, doubts and superstitions e'er they heard the welcome music of victory.

I would say, in conclusion, let every child study music, even though in this branch no special success attend him, it may awaken the mind to some branch in which *is* success. And the mind awakened to a love and appreciation of the æsthetic is being led to a knowledge of God. For such *is* the *mission of the æsthetic*, and these inspirations prove His presence. Many begin music and after a time drop it, believing they have failed. Not so. Though the recording angel has an immense book of good beginnings somewhere, which we will *all* have to help square up sometime, somehow, yet my faith tells me that these unfulfilled records may be counterbalanced by another of good endings where we started in one path and came out in another, and better one. To cultivate the æsthetic makes youth bright and beautiful, the prime of life more glorious, and is a fund of pure knowledge and faith from which age may draw, as the life-notes lose their gay appogiaturas, trills and runs, and retard slower and slower, and at last stop altogether as the inharmonious discord of death breaks in—just as a prelude to the wondrous psalm of eternal life. Ah, Pythagoras, there is the firm foundation of truth in thy wise philosophy, for truly when the final chord of peace is struck it is *not* lost or stilled in eternal silence, but swells the harmony of the music of the spheres.